QUEEN
ELIZABETH II

Sally Morgan

Illustrated by **Sarah Papworth**

SCHOLASTIC

Published in the UK by Scholastic , 2022
Euston House, 24 Eversholt Street, London, NW1 1DB
Scholastic Ireland, 89E Lagan Road, Dublin Industrial Estate,
Glasnevin, Dublin, D11 HP5F

Text © Sally Morgan, 2022
Illustrations by Sarah Papworth © Scholastic, 2022

ISBN 978 0702 31372 1

A CIP catalogue record for this book is available from the British Library.

Printed by CPI Group (UK) Ltd, Croydon, CR0 4YY
Paper made from wood grown in sustainable forests and other
controlled sources.

1 3 5 7 9 10 8 6 4 2

www.scholastic.co.uk

CONTENTS

THE MOST FAMOUS WOMAN IN THE WORLD

On 2 June 1953, a young woman named Elizabeth rode through the streets of London in a two-hundred-year-old golden coach. Elizabeth was on her way to take part in a ceremony that would be witnessed and capture the imaginations of millions of people all over the world. It was a ceremony that would change her life and the lives of her family, set her on a path to breaking many records, and transform her into the most famous woman in the world.

But why were Elizabeth and this ceremony considered so important? The ceremony was important, because it was Elizabeth's coronation – where she would be crowned 'Elizabeth the Second, by the Grace of God of the United Kingdom of Great Britain and Northern Ireland and of Her other Realms and Territories Queen, Head of the Commonwealth, Defender of the Faith.' It was a long title, but what did it all mean?

WHAT IT MEANS TO BE QUEEN

The United Kingdom has a monarchy, which means that a king or queen, known as the sovereign, is the head of state. Many years ago, this meant that the king or queen had the power to make laws, but today this power belongs to Parliament which is voted for by the people. This is called a Constitutional Monarchy. In the United Kingdom, although the government acts on behalf of the sovereign, in practice the king or queen cannot make laws. The sovereign is not allowed to be seen to be political in any way. Instead, laws are suggested by the government and passed by Parliament.

What are Realms and Territories?

It meant that Elizabeth was queen, not just

of the United Kingdom but of a group of countries known as 'realms'. These realms were independent countries that recognized the sovereign of the United Kingdom as their sovereign too. At the time of her coronation the realms of the Commonwealth included Canada, Australia, New Zealand, South Africa, Pakistan and Ceylon (now known as Sri Lanka).

Elizabeth was also queen in a number of British Territories. British Territories are countries overseas that are ruled by the United Kingdom, but are not a part of it. These territories were once part of the British Empire. In 1952, the United Kingdom had more than seventy British Territories.

Since the coronation, a number of countries, then considered British Territories, have become independent countries which recognize the queen as their head of state. Also, four countries – Pakistan, South Africa and Ceylon and Barbados became republics, meaning that they now have an elected president instead of a king or queen. Today Elizabeth is queen in fifteen Commonwealth realms.

What is Defender of the Faith?

The title of 'Defender of the Faith' has been held by every monarch since King Henry VIII. As Supreme Governor of the Church of England, Elizabeth has the power to appoint bishops, archbishops and church leaders. To do this Elizabeth takes the advice of the prime minister. After their appointment, church leaders are asked to swear an oath to the queen.

The historic coronation ceremony took place at Westminster Abbey, the place where every coronation ceremony for an English monarch has taken place since Christmas Day in 1066.

On Christmas Day 1066, Elizabeth's great grandfather, from twenty-nine generations ago, William the Conqueror, celebrated his coronation at a place called Edward's Abbey, that stood at the site of the current abbey. Edward's Abbey was rebuilt in the middle of the 13th century on the orders of King Henry III who died before its completion. As well as coronations, Westminster Abbey has hosted many royal weddings including Elizabeth's wedding to Philip Mountbatten in 1947.

Inside Westminster Abbey, politicians, church leaders, ambassadors, foreign dignitaries and members of the Royal Family waited for Elizabeth to arrive for her coronation ceremony.

Also waiting for Elizabeth was the man who would perform the ceremony, the Archbishop of Canterbury, Geoffrey Fisher. The coronation ceremony has been performed by the Archbishop of Canterbury for almost every king or queen of England since 1066. The Archbishop of Canterbury is the most senior bishop and spiritual leader of the Church of England and head of the Anglican Communion – one of the largest Christian communities in the world with members in 165 countries.

It was a historic ceremony in a historic setting. Elizabeth was taking part in a tradition that went back over 1,200 years. The role of queen was not a position she applied for, and it wasn't a job that was supposed to be hers, but ever since she was ten years old, she knew it was a duty that she would be expected to fulfil just as her father and all the kings and queens that had come before her had done so. But although Elizabeth knew she was taking her place in history as queen, she also knew that part of her duty was to make sure that position was relevant to people both in 1952 and well into the future.

Queen of the Future

Also waiting for Elizabeth's arrival were cameras, set up to film the ceremony for people to watch at home. It was the first time the ceremony was allowed to be filmed.

At the airport, aeroplanes stood by to carry film of the ceremony to countries all over the globe. Three separate flights were scheduled to Canada to take batches of film across the Atlantic as and when they became available. This would allow Canadians to watch the ceremony on the day it took place. Another copy of the film was put on a plane to Australia, where it landed 53 hours later. Flights with batches of film took off from London to land in the United States of America so television networks there could show the ceremony.

It is estimated that around 277 million people saw all or part of the ceremony, whether around a television in the comfort of their own homes or as part of newsreels shown before films at the cinema.

When Elizabeth entered the abbey, she was greeted by her maids of honour who had to carry her 5 metres-long (18 feet) embroidered velvet train. The maids of honour helped Elizabeth arrange her silk gown to prepare her to walk down the aisle. When they were finished, the music started and Elizabeth said, "Ready, girls?" Her maids of honour were ready, but was Elizabeth? She was about to find out.

Queen Elizabeth after her Coronation

After the ceremony, Elizabeth rode in her carriage back to Buckingham Palace. It had been a long day in which she had done her duty, met many new people and waved and smiled at thousands upon thousands of cheering people lining the streets.

BUCKINGHAM PALACE

Buckingham Palace has been the London home of the kings and queens of the United Kingdom since 1837.

The palace has 775 rooms, 52 royal and guest bedrooms and 188 bedrooms for staff who work in the palace. As well as being a home, Buckingham Palace houses 92 offices where administrators who organize the lives and duties of the Queen and the Royal Family work, and 19 state rooms where the Queen performs her duties. Buckingham Palace hosts

> 50,000 official visitors each year as guests to banquets, garden parties and audiences. Buckingham Palace is also a major tourist attraction with millions of people coming to visit the public spaces and rooms each year.

At the palace, Elizabeth appeared on the balcony with her family to wave to the crowd. All of her plans had worked perfectly. She had prepared for her coronation meticulously and over the last year she had rehearsed each moment. Elizabeth had helped organize every part of the day, from designing her silk gown to allowing and reviewing the position of the cameras in the abbey.

Elizabeth knew the world would be watching and she wanted them to, but deep down Elizabeth was a shy woman. She was a wife and a mother who loved nothing more than spending time in the countryside with her family, her horses and her dogs – but now she was also queen.

Down below the crowd looked up to see Elizabeth smiling, glittering in her crown and jewels and as they looked, many of them wondered what Queen Elizabeth was really like and what she would be like as their queen.

A LITTLE PRINCESS

On 21 April 1926, at 2.40 a.m., a very special little girl was born at 17 Bruton Street, London, to two excited parents. While many new parents refer to their baby girls as princesses, this little girl really was one. The baby's mother was Elizabeth, Duchess of York and her father was

Baby Elizabeth with her parents

Albert, Duke of York, son of King George V of the United Kingdom and Dominions and Emperor of India.

The little princess was given the name Elizabeth Alexandra Mary Windsor. Her parents named the child after her own mother, Elizabeth, her father's grandmother Queen Alexandra and her father's mother, Queen Mary.

Being named after two queens, one might think that Elizabeth's fate was sealed from the start, but the truth was far from it. Even though Elizabeth's grandfather was king, and her father was a duke, no one thought she would ever be a queen herself. This was because her father was second in line for the throne after his older brother David, Prince of Wales (Elizabeth's uncle). This made Princess Elizabeth third in line to the throne. Third in line doesn't sound too far away but if her uncle married and had children, his children would follow him on to the throne after he died.

But that wasn't all. Even if her uncle, the Prince of Wales, died leaving no children, and her father inherited the throne, Elizabeth would only follow him as queen if she did not have any brothers. This was due to a law which said that the crown passed to the monarch's first-born son when he died, whether or not this son had a much more sensible older sister.

But even though the little princess was unlikely to become queen, when officials at the palace announced Elizabeth's birth, newspapers around the world reported the good news and many went wild with princess fever.

The World's Most Famous Baby

As word spread of her birth, Princess Elizabeth soon became the world's most famous baby and people everywhere wanted to know more about her. Elizabeth was the first of a new generation of the Royal Family and, just as today, when a picture of a royal baby appeared in the newspaper, it caused quite a stir with people wanting to know exactly what the royal babies were wearing so that they could rush out and buy or make similar clothes for their little ones.

As a member of the royal family, Elizabeth was born into a happy home filled with privilege and wealth, but this wasn't the experience of everyone who lived in England at the time.

GREAT BRITAIN IN 1926

When Elizabeth was born, much of Great Britain was still suffering the aftereffects of the First World War.

The war cost a lot of money, and although the allies won, many people were left unable to find work. For those lucky enough to find jobs, working conditions were bad and the wages were so low that many people struggled to earn enough to feed their families. People who worked in coal mines suffered the most with their wages being cut almost in half. Many workers believed the government and business owners should do more to help people. On 4 May 1926, millions of people across the UK took part in what came to be known as the General Strike. A strike is where a group of workers decide together not to go to work, as a way of protesting about how they are treated by their employers.

To help stop the nation grinding to a halt, the government called in the armed forces to drive buses and do other jobs needed to keep the country moving.

George V had sympathy with the strikers and urged people to, 'Try living on their wages before you judge them.'

The strike lasted for nine days, but some people feared the action could lead to workers attempting to overthrow the government in a revolution, something that could be very dangerous for the royal family.

REVOLUTIONS AND ROYALTY

In 1917, nine years before Elizabeth's birth, King George V's cousin, Tsar Nicholas II of Russia, and his family were overthrown by revolutionaries and later murdered.

Revolutionaries were tired of poor working conditions and blamed the tsar and other wealthy people in Russia. They believed the labour and suffering of working people paid for the lavish lifestyles of the upper class and royal family, a class ordinary Russians could never expect to join. They hoped that by getting rid of the monarchy and establishing a new government and leadership, things would improve for ordinary people.

Thankfully for King George V, although he was related to the tsar he was a very different monarch, belonging to a very different kind of monarchy. Great Britain has what is known as a constitutional monarchy, which means unlike Tsar Nicholas II, who was in charge of everything, King George V had very little real power. Although, George was head of state, the power to make laws and all of the big decisions for the nation are made by Parliament, which is voted for by the people.

Princess Elizabeth was christened in a family ceremony at the chapel at Buckingham Palace on 19 May 1926. With so many people in the country suffering, George V didn't believe it was sensible to flaunt the royal family's wealth and privilege. As a leader, he believed he and his family should set an example to the people.

A Very Happy Home

While Elizabeth was christened in a palace, she didn't grow up in one. Buckingham Palace was where her grandfather, whom she called 'Grandpa England', George V lived with her grandmother,

Queen Mary. Instead, the young princess lived with her mother and father less than a mile down the road at 145 Piccadilly, London.

145 Piccadilly was a tall, narrow, terraced house with a walled garden. Elizabeth's room, or nursery, was on the top floor, where she slept in a cot lined with pink satin. Elizabeth, like most babies born into rich families at the time, shared her room with her nanny, a lady who had been hired to look after her. Elizabeth's nanny was called Clara Knight, but everyone called her 'Alah', because young Elizabeth couldn't pronounce her name. Elizabeth struggled to pronounce her own name too and referred to herself as 'Lillibet', a name that stuck with members of her family. Alah ran the nursery and along with her assistants, looked after Elizabeth's clothes and meals and put her to bed at night. She would also take Elizabeth out for walks in the park and to play in the gated garden opposite their home. Living in town could be difficult though; a lot of people were interested in the young princess and wanted to know more about her. Reporters would hide in bushes to get pictures and once

passers-by knew who she was, people started to gather, eager to get close to her.

As well as spending time in the city, the family also had a home in Richmond Park called White Lodge. Here Elizabeth and her nanny were able to go outside without being watched.

Although Elizabeth had a nanny, she still saw a lot of her parents. The Duke and Duchess of York, Albert and Elizabeth, were delighted with their new daughter and wanted to spend as much time with her as possible. The Duke was determined to make his daughter's childhood as happy as his was miserable.

HIS ROYAL HIGHNESS, PRINCE ALBERT, DUKE OF YORK

Prince Albert was a shy man, who hadn't enjoyed his childhood. As a young boy, Albert had to wear braces on his legs to help straighten them. Albert's parents, King George and Queen Mary, were often cold towards him and criticized him. They hired school-teachers who were cruel to him and forced him to write with his right hand although he was naturally left-handed. This made learning very difficult.

As well as struggling to write, the young prince had a speech impediment which caused him to stammer when he tried to talk. His stammer could be so bad that people struggled to understand what Albert was saying which would make him angry and frustrated.

George V made it very clear to Albert that he was not what he expected from a royal son and took very little interest in him. Instead, the King and Queen focused their attention on Albert's older brother, David.

While Prince Albert had an unhappy childhood, he was very happily married to his wife Elizabeth

Bowes-Lyon, who was the daughter of the Earl of Strathmore. Elizabeth was seen as an unconventional choice for a royal bride because, although she was the daughter of an earl, she was not the daughter of a European royal. The king had given his permission for the marriage because he did not believe his son was likely to be king and therefore his choice of wife wasn't of concern.

Unlike Albert, Elizabeth remembered having a very happy childhood, growing up on the east coast of Scotland. She was very close to her parents and wanted to have the same relationship with her children. Every morning the Duke and Duchess asked Alah to bring baby Elizabeth into their bedroom to play. They tried to be there for Elizabeth's bedtime and bath time which was often loud and full of splashing and giggles.

In many ways, they were just a normal (if very wealthy) family, and Elizabeth was just a normal little girl. Except she wasn't – she was royal. Her grandfather was the King of the United Kingdom, and even though it was unlikely that she would ever be queen herself, it did mean that her life was very different to other girls.

Elizabeth was recognized wherever she went and people often smiled and waved when they saw her. Some people even curtseyed or bowed. While most children travelled by bus or train, or rode their bicycles, Elizabeth travelled in limousines and the royal train and even beside the king in an open-topped carriage. On her birthdays or Christmas, people all over the world sent her cards and Christmas presents.

Grandpa England

Elizabeth's grandfather may not have been a very kind father, but King George V was a devoted grandfather. He enjoyed playing games with Elizabeth and helped to teach her how to deal with all of the attention she was getting. King George taught Elizabeth that it was important that she was always on her best behaviour as any bad mood or misstep would be reported in the papers and make her and her family look very bad. Instead, it was Elizabeth's duty to smile and be polite, as many people in the country were not as well off or lucky as she was and that if she looked unhappy, people would think she took all the privilege of being royal and a princess for granted.

The young princess spent time with her grandparents on her mother's side, too. The Duchess of York's family lived in a 15th century castle called Glamis Castle and the Duchess liked to visit them there with her daughter as often as she could.

GLAMIS CASTLE

Glamis Castle was built as a fortress in the 1370s. The red sandstone building has towers and turrets and as well as more than a few ghosts roaming the halls. Glamis Castle was also the home of Macbeth, the Scottish king whose story inspired one of playwright William Shakespeare's most famous plays. .

Glamis Castle

It was on a family holiday to Glamis Castle that Princess Elizabeth got a very special gift – a sister. Elizabeth's mother gave birth to Margaret Rose on 21 August 1930. Margaret's birth gave the castle another claim to fame as Princess Margaret's birthplace, the first royal to be born in Scotland since 1600.

Elizabeth was delighted. Now she had her very own playmate to join her in the nursery. Elizabeth loved her sister very much right away and was very protective of her. Elizabeth liked to push Margaret's pram when they went out with their nanny on walks and always made sure her sister was given whatever she was given so that Margaret didn't feel left out.

Horse Mad

Elizabeth was a clever girl and very well behaved, perhaps thanks to her grandfather's lessons. She was tidy too, and took great care in making sure all of her toys were put away properly.

Being a princess, Elizabeth had a lot of toys. Elizabeth's favourite toys were her collection of more than thirty wooden horses, each with its own saddle. Elizabeth took care of these horses as if they were real, brushing their manes and tails, taking off each of their saddles, and giving them food and water before she went to bed at night.

Wooden toy horse

Elizabeth liked to play horse with her nanny too, who let Elizabeth pretend she was a horse and they would pretend to run made-up errands and visit imaginary friends around the nursery.

When Elizabeth was four, her grandfather, King George V, gave her a very special Christmas present: a Shetland pony named Peggy. Elizabeth started riding lessons soon afterwards.

Shetland pony

Elizabeth's mother taught Elizabeth to read by the time she was just five years old and as soon as she was able to read books on her own, Elizabeth found she loved to read about horses, too... Her favourite book was *Black Beauty* by Anna Sewell.

By the time she was five Elizabeth could read and write well even though she didn't go to school. In the 1930s, many girls born into wealthy families didn't go to school, but were taught at home by a teacher called a governess instead. Elizabeth's mother and father hired a governess named Marion Crawford to come and teach the princess. Marion, who became known as 'Crawfie' to the family, taught Elizabeth, and eventually her little sister Margaret, everything they would otherwise learn at school. Crawfie, like most governesses, lived with the family in their home and travelled with them when they moved to different houses.

A Day in the Life

For Elizabeth, lessons began with Crawfie in the schoolroom at 9.30 a.m., after she had had her breakfast and chatted with her parents in their bedroom. Until Margaret was old enough, she stayed in the nursery with the nanny. Morning lessons consisted of maths, which they called arithmetic, grammar, history, writing and poetry, as well as thirty minutes of religious instruction.

At 11.00 a.m. they would take a break for a glass of orange juice and a walk around the gardens in the square outside their house. When they got back, it was quiet time, when Elizabeth was expected to lie down and either rest or read to herself before lunch.

Lunch was in the nursery when they were very little, but as they got older, Elizabeth and

Margaret were allowed to have lunch with their parents downstairs. After lunch they would have dance class, singing, drawing or music.

The girls had their tea in the nursery and then had bath time with their parents, or Alah. After bath it was time for a story and bed.

On Friday afternoons, the family would travel to their home in the countryside.

A New Home in the Country

When Elizabeth was five years old, her grandfather gave the Duke of York the use of a house called Royal Lodge, three miles from Windsor Castle. Nestled among the enormous trees and ornate gardens of Windsor Great Park, Royal Lodge was the perfect place for the young Duke and his family to retreat from the hustle and bustle of London and get some fresh air.

In London, it was hard to ensure that the princesses could play outside with privacy and safety. At Windsor they could explore the grounds to their hearts' content. But the weekends weren't just for playing. On Saturday mornings, Elizabeth had more lessons with Crawfie, revising what they had learned during the week. In the afternoons, Elizabeth got to go riding at the house's stables where they kept their horses.

On Sundays they went to church and spent time together as a family. There was no riding on a Sunday, but Elizabeth didn't mind because she thought that horses deserved a rest, too.

"IF I AM EVER QUEEN, I SHALL MAKE A LAW THAT THERE MUST BE NO RIDING ON SUNDAYS. HORSES SHOULD HAVE A REST TOO."

Princess Elizabeth, c.1931

The Little House of Windsor

As princesses, Elizabeth and her sister received lots of presents for their birthdays, many from people they hadn't even met. Most of those presents were given away, but they did get to keep some extra-special gifts. On Elizabeth's sixth birthday she got one of these gifts from the people of Wales. It was a playhouse, built in the grounds of Royal Lodge. The house was called *Y Bwthyn Bach*, which means 'The Little House' in Welsh and was a real princess-sized thatched cottage, with running water and electricity. The Little House had a working stove, a fridge, a kitchen sink and even a little bathroom. There was a second floor with bedrooms, wallpaper on the walls and curtains at the windows. It had everything a modern home at the time would have, in miniature. There were pots and pans and crockery and glasses.

Elizabeth and Margaret playing in the miniature cottage

Elizabeth and Margaret rushed to their playhouse whenever they went to Royal Lodge. They cooked and they cleaned and had fun rearranging the furniture. They took great care of it, making sure to pack everything away and cover the furniture with dust covers when they returned to London.

Puppy Love

Another special Welsh present Elizabeth received was a deep reddish-brown corgi given to her by her father the Duke of York in 1933. The word 'corgi' is Welsh for 'dwarf dog'. The young princess fell in love, and it was a love she would feel for the rest of her life. Elizabeth called her puppy Dookie. Whereas Elizabeth was known for being a very well-behaved little girl, her little dog was not. Dookie, like many corgis, had a loud piercing bark and liked nothing more than to nip people who annoyed him. Elizabeth thought he was very funny and soon Dookie was given a playmate named Jane. Dookie and Jane were the first of many corgis Elizabeth would own throughout her life. Elizabeth loved to take Dookie and Jane on walks and took care of them by herself.

corgi

With the ponies, puppies, playhouses and palaces, it's easy to think that Princess Elizabeth and her sister had everything they could possibly want, but they didn't. They longed for things ordinary children took for granted. For one thing, apart from each other, the young princesses didn't have many friends their own age. Instead they spent most of their time surrounded by grown-ups. They didn't go on many outings either, and when they did they were treated as 'special guests' and not normal children. When they visited London Zoo they didn't just buy a ticket and join a crowd to go through the turnstiles with their mum and dad like everyone else. Instead, the zoo was closed for a private visit where the princesses were invited to meet all of the animals and pet them.

Penguins at London Zoo

If they went to a pantomime, which they did once a year, instead of sitting with everyone else in front of the stage, they had to sit in the Royal Box. In theatres, the Royal Box is high up and far off to one side and the girls had to lean over the side to be able to see. The princesses wished they could be part of the fun and sit with the people in the seats below.

They wanted to travel like ordinary children, too. Riding in limousines and horse-drawn coaches may sound glamorous, but the girls got lonely. They wished they could crush in with everyone else on the underground train or bus. Elizabeth and Margaret begged their governess to take them, and Crawfie agreed, but they couldn't just hop on the train. The whole outing had to be carefully planned and they had to take a member of the household security to make sure nothing happened to them.

Going out for Royal Tea

For the girls this was more of an adventure than a trek through the wilderness would have been. At the station they bought their own tickets themselves from their pocket money and rode on an escalator, holding the handrail tightly. They travelled on the Tube from Hyde Park Corner to Tottenham Court Road to the Young Women's Christian Association (YWCA) where they had tea. As princesses, Elizabeth and Margaret were used to their tea being served to them on an elegant silver tray, but at the YWCA they had to queue up for it and pour it themselves.

The girls were thrilled walking the streets and imagined what it would be like to have an ordinary life. But the reason they couldn't do these things soon became apparent when someone recognized the young pair and a crowd started to gather, eager to get close to them. While no one meant any harm, the crushing people could have soon become dangerous, so the detective who had accompanied them put in an urgent call for a car. When it arrived, Elizabeth and Margaret were rushed back to their home in Piccadilly.

A Normal Little Girl

While her life was sometimes extraordinary, Elizabeth was like any other girl. She could be shy but sometimes let her temper get the better of her, once tipping an inkwell over Princess Margaret's head. Elizabeth bit her nails and no matter how hard Crawfie tried, she couldn't get her to stop. Elizabeth was encouraged when she saw the prime minister Neville Chamberlain have a cheeky chew on his own nails and reasoned that if it was good enough for a prime minister it was good enough for her.

Neville Chamberlain

While they certainly weren't perfect, Elizabeth and Margaret delighted their mother and father and the four of them were very close. The girls worked hard with their governess and knew how to behave whenever they had important guests such as their grandparents, King George V and Queen Mary, who came to visit them often. King George loved his granddaughters very much, but as he got older his health began to fail. King George suffered from lung problems caused by his many years of smoking. This meant he was unable to play with his grandchildren as he used to.

A Handsome Prince

One visitor who was young enough to play with the girls was their Uncle Edward, their father's older brother. Uncle Edward, otherwise known as the Prince of Wales, was heir to the throne. Most of the family, including the princesses, called him David. He had blonde hair and blue eyes and was considered very good-looking. As a handsome young prince, the newspapers were filled with stories trying to guess when and who he would pick to be his wife. King George V was getting older and people were becoming impatient as to when the young prince would settle down.

Unlike his brother, David was destined to be king and so whomever he married would one day be queen. Because of this, it was speculated that David would follow tradition and marry a foreign princess or someone from a noble, preferably royal family. Once he had married his royal bride, they were expected to have children, the eldest (male) of which would become king after he died. David had grown up knowing his future was predetermined and that his choice of wife would not just affect the rest of his life, but the lives of everyone in his family and the country. King George V was impatient to see David settle down too, worried that if the prince delayed he could bring a scandal on the family.

But George V never got to see the Prince of Wales marry. At the beginning of 1936, the king fell ill while staying at Sandringham. On 20 January 1936, after twenty-six years on the throne he died, aged seventy. The next day, Elizabeth's uncle, the Prince of Wales, was proclaimed king.

NAME AND NUMBER

In the United Kingdom, when a monarch inherits the throne, he or she is allowed to choose whether they would like to keep the name given at birth or whether they would like to select a new one; this name is called his or her regnal name. The monarch's name is then followed by a number, written in Roman numerals. This number is known as a regnal number and sets the monarch apart from kings or queens that came before them who had the same name.

When Elizabeth's uncle became king, he chose the regnal name Edward, which made him King Edward VIII. This was the name that was printed on all of the new stamps, that was cast on to new post boxes and minted on coins. It was the name printed on commemorative souvenirs made in preparation for the new king's coronation. But the coronation never happened.

An Unsuitable Queen

Shortly after the proclamation, newspapers started mentioning a glamorous American woman named Mrs Wallis Simpson as a guest at the new king's home. For a while nobody thought anything of it. But as the mentions became more regular, many began to wonder if King Edward and Mrs Simpson were more than friends. They were. The new king had fallen in love with Mrs Simpson and wanted to marry her. This was a problem, because as king, Edward's choice of bride was not just his own. It had to be approved by the British government. Edward was expected to marry a woman of noble birth and

Mrs Simpson was not, but this wasn't the only problem. Mrs Simpson had been married twice before. The government did not approve. Not only this, as king, Edward would become head of the Church of England which did not allow people to remarry after divorce. The Church of England did not officially permit remarriage after divorce until 2002.

The government gave Edward an ultimatum: either he could be king or marry Mrs Simpson; he could not have both. Edward chose Mrs Simpson.

A Never-Crowned King

On 11 December 1936, less than a year after he was proclaimed king, Edward VIII gave a speech announcing that he was stepping down from (known as 'abdicating') the throne.

"A FEW HOURS AGO, I DISCHARGED MY LAST DUTY AS KING AND EMPEROR, AND

"NOW THAT I HAVE BEEN SUCCEEDED BY MY BROTHER, THE DUKE OF YORK, MY FIRST WORDS MUST BE TO DECLARE MY ALLEGIANCE TO HIM. THIS I DO WITH ALL MY HEART."

King Edward VIII, 1936

The Duke of York, Elizabeth's father, was proclaimed king the very next day and his quiet, happy life and the little world he had built for his family would never be the same again.

A NEW KING

The abdication of King Edward VIII meant a lot of changes for Elizabeth's whole family. One of the first changes for Albert was his name. After his brother rejected the throne, Albert wanted to show the country that they could rely on him, and that he would be as good to them as his father had, and so rather than becoming King Albert, he took George as his regnal name, becoming King George VI. Elizabeth's mother became queen consort.

Elizabeth didn't attend the special ceremony called the proclamation, where her father officially became king, but she realized how much their lives were going to change as soon as her father returned home. Instead of running to her father and hugging him, as she was used to doing, now, as king, Elizabeth and her sister were expected to curtsy before him. Before the abdication, Elizabeth had spent a great deal of time with her mother and father, running into the bedroom each morning, seeing them at mealtimes and saying goodnight, but now her father was king, their lives would be very different.

From the moment he was proclaimed king, Elizabeth's father had to take on the role and responsibilities of the monarch. This meant performing many more official duties, such as spending hours reading and signing government papers that were delivered each day. As king he also had audiences with the prime minister to discuss how the government was doing. On top of all of this, his diary was filled with all the official engagements he was expected to attend, such as the Trooping of the Colour and the State Opening of Parliament. Elizabeth's father and mother would also have to represent the British government abroad and go on extended tours to visit British Territories overseas.

Problems at the Palace

Albert becoming king would also mean a new home for Elizabeth. As king, her father would be expected to receive world leaders as guests and host lavish banquets and parties. 145 Piccadilly was a beautiful house, but it wasn't suitable for that.

Instead, Elizabeth and her family moved into Buckingham Palace and she wasn't happy about it. To Elizabeth and her family, Buckingham Palace was intimidating and gloomy. It had always been where her grandparents lived, and therefore meant getting dressed up in their best clothes and being on their best behaviour. It came with miles of corridors, hundreds of staff, and mice! It was nothing like her comfortable home at 145 Piccadilly, or Royal Lodge. Elizabeth thought it was going to need some changes if they were to be happy there.

An Unlikely King

Elizabeth's father had never wanted to be king. He was shy and wasn't good at public speaking due to his stammer. Some people thought he might not even show up to his own coronation, but he did. Although it was not the future that he wanted, George felt it was his duty and on 12 May 1937, George VI was crowned king at

Westminster Abbey. Thousands of people lined the streets in the hope of seeing the new king riding in a golden horse-drawn carriage with his queen consort. They hoped to catch a glimpse of the little princesses too. Elizabeth and Margaret attended the ceremony. Elizabeth wrote that she had found much of the ceremony rather dull but was delighted by the silk dresses and real crowns she and Margaret got to wear, and the feast afterwards with delicious sandwiches and orangeade.

After the ceremony was over, Margaret asked Elizabeth an important question.

Margaret: Does this mean you will one day be Queen?

Elizabeth: Yes. I suppose it does.

Margaret: Poor you.

THE CORONATION

In the United Kingdom, a person officially becomes king or queen at the time of their proclamation which happens shortly after the death of the previous monarch. The new king or queen does not have a coronation right away. The coronation of a new king or queen takes place a number of months after the death of the previous king or queen, to allow time for the funeral as well as a period of mourning. A coronation is a religious ceremony in which a sovereign is crowned and where he or she swears the Coronation Oath.

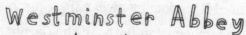

In Great Britain, the coronation of a king or queen takes place at Westminster Abbey in London and has done for over 900 years.

The ceremony has changed very little during that time. The ceremony is conducted by the Archbishop of Canterbury who is the spiritual leader of the Church of England.

In the first part of the ceremony, the Archbishop of Canterbury calls on everyone in the abbey to recognize the rightful king or queen before them.

After this the king or queen promises to serve the United Kingdom by swearing something called the Coronation Oath. In the Coronation Oath, the king or queen promises:

• To govern the peoples of the United Kingdom of Great Britain and Northern Ireland, and the dominions according to their respective laws and customs;

• To cause law and justice in mercy to be executed in all judgments, to their power;

- To maintain and preserve the Church of England, and its doctrine, worship, discipline and government as by law established in England;

- To preserve the rights and privileges of the bishops and clergy of England.

After swearing the oath, the sovereign signs it. The archbishop then performs a traditional Church of England ceremony called a Communion Service.

A canopy is held over the sovereign's head as they sit while the archbishop anoints him or her with holy oil.

After the anointing the sovereign is given the Coronation regalia. The regalia are precious objects that symbolize the king or queen's power and majesty.

The regalia includes:

The Sovereign's Orb: a golden orb topped with a jewelled cross. The orb symbolizes the sovereign's role as Head of the Church of England. The Sovereign's Orb is placed in the sovereign's right hand before being returned to the altar.

The Coronation Ring: the coronation ring is placed on the sovereign's right hand and is a symbol of dignity.

Sovereign's Sceptre with Cross: symbolizes the king or queen's power. The Sovereign's Sceptre is topped with the Cullinan 1 diamond, an enormous 530.2 carat diamond thought to be the largest cut diamond in the world.

Rod of Equity and Mercy: a gold rod topped with an enamel dove. Symbolizes the king or queen's role in caring for and leading his or her people with equity and mercy.

After receiving the regalia, it is time for the crowning. The Archbishop of Canterbury places the St Edward's crown on the sovereign's head.

The congregation then cries, "Long live the king!" (or queen).

A New Future for Elizabeth

Before the abdication, Elizabeth's parents had wanted each of their girls to have a fun and happy childhood before falling in love with a well-born young man and starting her own family. Now Elizabeth's father was king, as his eldest child Elizabeth's future was no longer the one they had planned for her. While Elizabeth could still become a wife and mother, when her father died, she would become queen.

With a very different future now ahead of her, Elizabeth's parents decided she needed a very different education – an education fit for a queen. Elizabeth had to learn about how Britain was run. As queen, Elizabeth would one day be head of the government and head of the army and head of the church, and as such, Elizabeth would be expected to meet regularly with the Prime Minister and discuss what was happening in Parliament and around the nation. For this she would need to know how all of it all worked.

She would not only be head of Great Britain; she would also be the head of the Commonwealth of Nations: the remains of an empire that had once covered more than a quarter of the world. She would be expected to visit and host world leaders. For this Elizabeth would need to learn about all of the countries of this empire and what it meant to be its figurehead.

To help with her education, her mother and father asked a teacher named Henry Marten, from Eton College, to come and teach her. While this might sound very serious, Henry Marten managed to make it interesting. He was known to be a little odd, keeping sugar lumps in his pockets and occasionally chewing on his handkerchief.

With Henry, Elizabeth learned all about how, in the past, British sailors had travelled all over the globe and claimed the land as British, even though people already lived there. They claimed so much land for the British that it became the biggest empire the world had ever seen, stretching from Australia to Canada and including much of Asia and Africa. Elizabeth learned how people native to these countries didn't always want to be ruled by the British and that by 1939 many of these countries had their own governments. These places, formerly known as colonies, were now referred to as dominions and formed a union of nations called the Commonwealth of Nations.

WHAT IS THE COMMONWEALTH?

The king or queen of Great Britain is also the head of something called the Commonwealth of Nations. The Commonwealth of Nations is a group of countries, almost all of which were once part of the British Empire who now

Commonwealth flag

govern themselves but who choose to maintain a relationship with Britain and each other. Rather than being ruled by Britain these countries formed an alliance of independent and equal nations.

These were all very advanced subjects for a girl of her age and unlike anything any other girl in England would have been taught at the time.

After-school Activities

In Elizabeth's lessons both with her teachers and her father, she learned about the life of duty

Unemployment in Germany skyrocketed, and many people couldn't afford food or a place to live.

Hitler and the Nazis rose to power by promising people an end to these hard times. They promised to abolish the Treaty of Versailles and to make Germany, then a republic of different states, into a strong united nation under a single powerful ruler. The Nazis blamed many of Germany's problems on people whom they did not consider to be real Germans, such as Jewish people living in the country. Hitler and the Nazis believed German people were superior to other people and that the German population could grow into a great empire, but to do this they needed more space. Hitler's plan, which he had described in books written in the 1920s, was to invade much of Europe and by doing so take control of European territory overseas.

Hitler's plans were no secret. He made powerful speeches to his followers outlining his ideas for the German people. Many outside of Germany didn't like what they heard. They feared Germany was preparing for a war similar to the First World War, which had devasted the globe from 1914 to 1918 and cost nearly 20 million lives. To prevent this, the British, French and the Soviet Union (now known as Russia) governments agreed that they would come to one another's aid should Germany attack. These countries became known as the Allies. They hoped their strong alliance would deter Germany from making a move. Germany formed a similar agreement with Italy which became known as the Axis Alliance.

In March 1938, German troops marched into Austria and took control of the government. Many in Europe feared that this was just the beginning and that Germany had plans to invade other countries – they were right.

Two Life-Saving Missions

For now, Elizabeth's life carried on as normal, and in June 1939, Elizabeth won a life-saving swimming award – Children's Challenge Shield from the Royal Life-Saving Society. Elizabeth's parents, however, weren't there to see it. They had travelled to the USA and Canada on a life-saving mission of a very different kind. The tour was to visit important sites but also to visit more important friends. The royal couple hoped that by visiting they could secure the promise of help if war became unavoidable.

President Roosevelt

When they returned home, they toured the United Kingdom to show their support for people who were helping the country get ready for what might be to come. They took Elizabeth and Margaret with them on some of these trips.

A Brief Encounter

In July 1939, the Royal Family visited the Royal Naval College at Dartmouth on the south coast of England, on the royal yacht. While they were there, Elizabeth met a young sea cadet named Philip. Philip was such a good sailor that he had been chosen by the college to show the young princesses around; he was also very handsome. Philip was young and energetic, and kept Elizabeth and Margaret entertained by playing games with them. He had such a good time that he made a joke of trying to row after the royal yacht as the Royal Family sailed away.

Elizabeth had enjoyed visiting the naval college and even though she was only thirteen years old, she knew she liked Philip. He had been good fun and very kind to her and her sister and so when she sent him a letter to thank him, she was delighted when he wrote back.

GREAT BRITAIN
GOES TO WAR

In September 1939, the war everyone in Great Britain hoped could be avoided became a reality. After having broken numerous agreements, Germany and the Nazis invaded Poland. It was clear that Hitler was putting the plans he had written about in his books and boasted about in his speeches into action. Not only this, Hitler had allies too, in the shape of Italy and Japan. The British government felt they had no option but to declare war.

On the afternoon of 3 September 1939, Elizabeth's father made a speech to the nation over the radio.

"In this grave hour, perhaps the most fateful in our history, I send to every household of my peoples, both at home and overseas, this message, spoken with the same depth of feeling for each one of you as if I were able to cross your threshold and speak to you myself. For the second time in the lives of most of us we are at war."

It was a war that was going to affect the lives of everyone across Europe and many people around the world. On the same day that the British and the Allies declared war on Germany, so did Australia, New Zealand, India and Tonga from the Commonwealth, all promising to send troops and supplies to help. By 10 September, South Africa and Canada had done the same. The United States government had decided that they did not want to fight another war overseas after the First World War and had resolved to stay neutral.

For many men in the United Kingdom, going to war would mean going to fight. In 1939, all able-bodied men between the ages of eighteen and forty-one were expected to sign up at their local military office to join the army, navy or air force. Many had already done so, but when war was declared the need became even greater. After signing up, these men, many of whom had no military experience, were sent for basic training before going overseas to fight.

After invading Poland to the east, Hitler looked to the north, invading Denmark and Norway before setting his sights on the west. In May and June the Nazi troops marched through Luxembourg, Belgium, the Netherlands and on into France. As they marched they met fierce resistance, but the Allied troops were unable to hold them back and soon Germany occupied much of Northern France and the Atlantic coast in the south. Although they had fought bravely, the Allied troops had no choice but to retreat. Between 26 May and 4 June 1940 nearly 225,000 British and 114,000 Allied troops in France were evacuated from the French port of Dunkirk across the English Channel to the south coast of England.

With Hitler's Nazi troops making such quick progress across Europe, many feared that an invasion of the British mainland would be next. People also feared attack from the air as the Nazi air force sent aircraft loaded with bombs across the Channel to bomb targets around the country. With the land war in France won, Hitler turned his attentions east towards the Soviet Union, drawing up plans to invade – plans he put into action in December 1941.

THE BLITZ

Between September 1940 and May 1941, the Nazi air force, known as the Luftwaffe, dropped thousands of bombs on towns and cities all over the United Kingdom killing an estimated 43,500 people and injuring many more. This was known as the Blitz. The Luftwaffe chose cities in the hope of destroying strategic targets such as arms factories and airfields; they also hoped the repeated bombing would destroy morale and lead to a quick surrender from the British.

God Save the King

King George VI was given the option of taking himself and his family to safety overseas, but he refused. George felt that it was his duty to stay and stand alongside the people of Great Britain. As a king he was a symbol of the nation's strength and the idea of him sailing away in the face of danger would look like Britain was scared and sure of defeat. Instead the King and Queen remained at Buckingham Palace, London for much of the war.

His daughters however were a different matter. Like millions of children living in cities around the United Kingdom Elizabeth and Margaret were evacuated to the countryside. Unlike the other millions of children, Elizabeth and Margaret had their very own castle, Windsor, to retreat to.

Elizabeth Under Threat

To protect the young princesses from the air raids on Britain's major cities they were sent to Windsor Castle. Windsor Castle was a fortress, with thick stone walls, and was felt to be the safest place for them.

For extra safety, Elizabeth and Margaret's location was kept a secret for much of the war, the papers saying only that they had been sent to 'a house in the country'. As heir to the throne,

Elizabeth was believed to be a target for the Nazis because they hoped to restore her Uncle David – Edward VIII – to the throne, where they would make him do Germany's bidding.

Elizabeth and Margaret had visited Windsor Castle many times. It was usually a very grand place, filled with beautiful art and chandeliers. During the war, it looked very different. The castle staff covered the tall, leaded windows with thick, black drapes to prevent light from inside being seen from the air; they turned all the sparkling glass cabinets to face the walls and packed away all the treasures they contained. They even took down the chandeliers. Before the war, the castle walls were lined with paintings but now there were just empty frames as the precious art was removed and stored at a secret location, in case the Nazis invaded and targeted the castle.

Just like children all over the country, Elizabeth and Margaret had a lot to get used to but thankfully their nannies, Alah and Bobo, and their governess, Crawfie, went with them and did their best to keep them safe and entertained.

A Dark and Dingy Dungeon

Like any good fortress, Windsor Castle came
equipped with its very own dungeons which
were turned into an air-raid shelter. When the
siren sounded, Elizabeth and Margaret put their
coats over their pyjamas and padded down to the
dungeon with Alah and Bobo. They were then
expected to settle down on mattresses laid on
the floor, but no one got any sleep. They were
too frightened. At the beginning of the war, the
dungeons were far from luxurious. They were
dark and gloomy and were filled with beetles.
To help cheer them up, as the war went on, the
reinforced walls were given a bright coat of paint
and furnished more comfortably with bedrooms
for the princesses and the king and queen and
filled with toys and games to play with if they
had to be in the dungeon for a long time.

A Bomb at Buckingham Palace

While it was hard for Elizabeth and Margaret to
be away from their parents, it was the safest place

for them. From late August 1940, thousands of bombs were dropped in nightly raids on cities up and down the country including London and even Buckingham Palace itself. On the night of 13 September 1940, a bomb dropped by the Luftwaffe exploded at Buckingham Palace. Thankfully the King and Queen were unharmed, but a nearby workman was killed.

Elizabeth and Margaret did their best to get used to their new home but they knew that, although times were hard, they were very lucky. They had Crawfie, Alah and Bobo to look after them and their parents joined them whenever they could.

It was a frightening time for everyone, but especially children. They worried about themselves, about their mothers left in the cities and many worried about their fathers who had been sent abroad to fight.

On the Radio

To help reassure children who were frightened and homesick, the palace decided that Elizabeth should make her very first radio broadcast to the children of Great Britain and the Commonwealth of Nations. Elizabeth was very nervous; she worked on her speech with her mother and was reassured to have her sister by her side. On 13 October 1940, Elizabeth's speech was broadcast after a programme called Children's Hour.

"THOUSANDS OF YOU IN THIS COUNTRY HAVE HAD TO LEAVE YOUR HOMES AND BE SEPARATED FROM YOUR FATHERS AND MOTHERS. MY SISTER MARGARET ROSE AND I FEEL SO MUCH FOR YOU AS WE KNOW FROM EXPERIENCE WHAT IT MEANS TO BE AWAY FROM THOSE WE LOVE MOST OF ALL."

Princess Elizabeth, 1940

Not wanting her little sister to feel left out, when she had finished, Elizabeth called on her to wish everyone goodnight by saying,

"COME ON, MARGARET."

The War at Windsor

Thankfully the girls had plenty to keep themselves busy. As well as their lessons, they were able to ride, and re-form their Girl Guide pack with children from local families and those who had been evacuated nearby. Together they camped out in the grounds of Windsor Castle and learned new skills to earn badges.

Gas Mask Games

If you've seen pictures of children during the war, you may have seen them wearing gas masks. These gas masks were given to all adults and children in Great Britain to be used if the

Nazis dropped poisoned gas during their attacks. People were advised to wear them for ten or more minutes a day to get used to them. Elizabeth and Margaret had Mickey Mouse masks that they thought made them look like the monkeys they had seen at the zoo. They didn't like wearing them one bit, so they turned it into a game, running through the woods around the castle pretending to be monsters.

Gas mask

The Show Must Go On

At Christmastime, the girls were disappointed that they weren't able to go to their annual pantomime because, not only was it not safe for them to travel to London, but most of the theatres had closed during the war. Instead they put on pantomimes themselves. They made costumes and wrote scripts and designed posters which they hung up in the empty frames that lined the walls. They sold tickets to their friends and family to raise money for a war charity and invited soldiers who were stationed nearby. Margaret loved to perform and although Elizabeth could be shy, she enjoyed it too.

One of their shows when Elizabeth was fifteen had a very special guest of honour: the young sea cadet from the Royal Naval College at Dartmouth, Philip. When war broke out, Philip used his training to serve with the Royal Navy. He was a brave seaman who fought in many battles. Elizabeth and Philip had stayed in touch by writing letters to one another.

Philip was just as much fun as Elizabeth remembered and even more handsome. The King and Queen liked Philip, but they thought as Elizabeth was only fifteen it was too soon for her to be thinking about romance.

A WORLD WAR

As well as fighting in Europe, Allied troops
were sent to countries in Africa and Asia.
This was because Hitler and the Nazis wanted
to take control of Allied territories overseas.
In addition to the threat posed by the Nazis,
the Japanese Imperial Army were also on the
move in Asia. Like the Germans, the Japanese
wanted to expand their territory and occupy
land rich in precious resources such as coal,
oil and iron. In 1937, the Japanese Imperial
Army invaded China, after which the Emperor
set his sights on the Philippines, Malaya (now
Malaysia) and Indochina (now Vietnam and
Laos). On 27 September 1940, Japan formed
an alliance with Germany and Italy. On 7 and
8 December 1941 the Japanese Imperial Army
launched almost simultaneous attacks on the
Philippines, Indochina, Malaya, Hong Kong,
Singapore and Pearl Harbor in Hawaii, USA.

The bombing of Pearl Harbor killed 2,400 Americans and wounded 1,200 more. Shortly after the attack, the United States government declared war on Japan, forcing Japanese allies, Germany and Italy, to declare war on the US. For the United States the war was no longer overseas.

A WORKING ROYAL

In 1942, Elizabeth celebrated her sixteenth birthday. At sixteen girls became eligible to volunteer for war work. Elizabeth liked caring for people and wanted to volunteer as a nurse at a military hospital, but her father forbade it, believing it too dangerous for her. Instead her father made her an honorary colonel of a regiment called the Grenadier Guards. It was a great honour – as an honorary colonel she would get to inspect the troops, but she wouldn't get to fight or perform any real war work like women up and down the country were doing.

WOMEN AT WAR

With so many men overseas fighting, the government asked women to take up jobs traditionally done by men. Women were needed to work in the fields harvesting crops, drive buses and work in factories that made weapons. Women were also needed to work in the armed forces in jobs such as vehicle mechanics, air-raid wardens and searchlight operators. During the Second World War more than 640,000 women served with either the Women's Royal Naval Service, the Women's Auxiliary Air Force or the Auxiliary Territorial Service. By mid-1943 more than eighty per cent of women between the ages of twenty and thirty were involved in war work.

Doing Her Bit

In 1944, Elizabeth joined the women's branch of the British Army called the Auxiliary Territorial Service (ATS). In 1944, women were not permitted to fight, but were given roles as cooks, radar and searchlight operators, and drivers of military vehicles. Her father insisted that even though Elizabeth was heir to the throne she should not be given any special treatment. Instead she got her hands dirty with the rest of the recruits.

Elizabeth chose to train to become a mechanic, and worked hard learning how to strip engines and change tyres and even how to drive a lorry. Elizabeth qualified in April 1945. In her uniform and overalls Elizabeth looked unlike any princess Great Britain had ever seen. The press nicknamed her 'Princess Auto Mechanic'. Elizabeth spent most days at the ATS training base near Windsor but slept at the castle at night.

Elizabeth also learned how much effort people made preparing for royal visits, when her mother and father came to see her at work.

"I NEVER KNEW THERE WAS QUITE SO MUCH ADVANCE PREPARATION."

Princess Elizabeth, 1945

Duty Calls

This was an important lesson for Elizabeth because, now she was eighteen, Elizabeth began to take on more royal duties, opening wings of public buildings, such as museums and hospitals, handing out diplomas and attending events on behalf of her mother and father. She even gave speeches.

Although Elizabeth was shy, she soon got so used to meeting new people every single day that it became ordinary to her, but for the people she was meeting it was a chance of a lifetime.

Elizabeth always tried to remember an important piece of advice her father gave her: that as a princess, and one day a queen, people would remember meeting her and what she said for the rest of their lives. It was important for her to look interested and happy and never act as though she disapproved of anything.

A Long-Awaited Victory

Germany was fighting a war on two fronts: against the Soviet Union in the east and against the Allied forces, joined by the United States, in the west. As time passed it proved more and more difficult not only to fight but to keep their troops supplied with everything they needed to keep going. On 6 June 1944, Allied forces crossed the English Channel to invade Europe. They faced heavy fire, but pushed on and by the end of April 1945 the Allied forces had liberated Western Europe from German control. The Allied forces chased the Nazis from the west as Soviet forces forced them from the east, taking the German capital Berlin. With nowhere to turn, Germany surrendered and on 8 May 1945 Victory in Europe was declared. Elizabeth's father made a speech over the radio.

"SPEAKING FROM OUR EMPIRE'S OLDEST CAPITAL CITY, WAR-BATTERED BUT NEVER FOR ONE MOMENT DAUNTED OR DISMAYED – SPEAKING FROM LONDON, I ASK YOU TO JOIN

WITH ME IN THAT ACT OF THANKSGIVING. GERMANY, THE ENEMY WHO DROVE ALL EUROPE INTO WAR, HAS BEEN FINALLY OVERCOME."

King George VI, 1945

King George VI thanked all those who had fought so hard for this moment and gave special thanks for the servicemen and women and civilians who had fought bravely and lost their lives to make victory possible.

Crowds of people gathered outside Buckingham Palace, all wanting to see and celebrate with the Royal Family who had stayed with them through all their suffering and worry. The King and Queen did not disappoint; they stepped out on to the balcony to wave with Elizabeth, wearing her ATS uniform, at their side. Elizabeth wanted to celebrate with the crowd, and she did.

As people revelled and sang in the street, the

king allowed Elizabeth and Margaret to join them. The two princesses pulled down their hats so that they could slip into the crowd unnoticed and sing songs such as 'Roll Out the Barrel' and 'Run Rabbit Run'. It was a rare escape from royal life. It was a time of great celebration, but while the war was over in Europe, the fighting still raged in Asia and the Pacific.

The soldiers in the Pacific saw some of the worst fighting and conditions seen anywhere in the Second World War and suffered mass casualties from combat and disease. The United States was determined to end the war as quickly as possible.

On 6 August 1945, the United States Air Force dropped an atomic bomb on the city of Hiroshima in Japan. The bomb exploded killing sixty to eighty thousand people instantly, and thousands more with the toxic radiation it released into the atmosphere. United States President Harry Truman warned that unless the Japanese surrendered there would be more to come. The president was true to his word. Three days later the United States Air Force dropped a second, even more powerful, atomic bomb on the

Japanese city of Nagasaki killing 40,000 people instantly and many more from radiation caused by the explosion.

The sheer devastation caused by the two bombs left the Japanese with little choice. On 15 August 1945, Japan's ruler Emperor Hirohito announced his unconditional surrender over the radio. Victory over Japan was declared.

Six long and hard years after the war began, it was over. Once again King George VI thanked all the brave men and women who had fought so bravely to bring the conflict to a close.

"FROM THE BOTTOM OF MY HEART I THANK MY PEOPLE FOR ALL THEY HAVE DONE, NOT ONLY FOR THEMSELVES BUT FOR MANKIND."

King George VI, 1945

And once again Elizabeth and her sister slipped out to celebrate with the crowd.

A RIGHT ROYAL ROMANCE

Elizabeth had been only thirteen years old when the war began but now she was a young woman with a full-time job as a working royal.

Some of Elizabeth's public duties included becoming the head, or patron, of charities and societies. This gave the princess time and opportunity to explore some of her interests. It was good for the societies she represented too, as there was no better way to raise money than having the future queen speak at your functions and attend your events. Elizabeth became president of many societies including the Royal College of Music, as well as charities that cared for the needs of sick people and animals. Elizabeth felt it was important that these organizations were given the recognition they deserved for all the hard work they did helping people. And people needed help.

Great Britain and her allies were no longer at

war, but after the celebrations, it soon became clear that there was a long road ahead. Repeated bombings had destroyed many homes and buildings in cities all over the country. Many people struggled to find work and earn enough money to feed their families and even when they did have money, food was still in short supply and was, like many other things such as clothing and fuel, still very heavily rationed.

As Elizabeth's official work increased, so did her staff. She had secretaries to reply to her letters and organize her diary, and ladies-in-waiting to travel with her and organize her wardrobe. To accommodate her growing staff, Elizabeth had her own section of Buckingham Palace put aside for her. After the long quiet days at Windsor Castle, Elizabeth now had a public life that was busy and filled with engagements. Her private life was exciting too.

A Proper Proposal

After the war, Philip became a regular visitor to Elizabeth and her family, and it wasn't long until the young couple were very much in love.

Philip was a good match for Elizabeth; he was young and handsome, he had fought bravely during the war, and he was royal, being a member of both the Greek and Danish royal families. But Philip was not everybody's first choice as a match for Elizabeth. Many thought he wasn't serious enough to marry the future queen. When visiting Elizabeth and her family at Balmoral (see page 169), Philip wore a traditional kilt and thought it would be a good joke to curtsy, instead of bow before the king, as though he was a woman wearing a skirt. Philip was only being silly but some people thought this was disrespectful. But Philip's silliness wasn't the only problem.

Although Philip had fought bravely in the Royal Navy, many people questioned his loyalty to Great Britain because he had a number of powerful relatives who lived in Germany. Some suspected that Philip was dangerous and wanted to marry Elizabeth because he was a spy.

But Elizabeth was in love, and her family knew her mind was made up. When Elizabeth was twenty years old, Philip asked King George VI for his permission to marry her. King George agreed but he wanted to them to wait. The king believed that with the country having been through so much, it wasn't appropriate for them to hold a big elaborate wedding so soon after the war. He also wanted to spend more time together as a family before Elizabeth married and to give her a chance to see more of the world. King George knew that Elizabeth would one day be, not only Queen of the United Kingdom of Great Britain and Northern Ireland, but also Head of the Commonwealth which, thanks to the war, she had seen very little of.

As well as doing his duty as king, Elizabeth's father knew it was important to prepare Elizabeth for her life as queen after he died. George had not had the chance to do this with his own father, and he wanted Elizabeth to feel more prepared than he had been. Elizabeth had sat with her father as he looked through the parliamentary papers and they had discussed stories in the newspapers together, but she had never had the chance to see any of the vast territory she would one day preside over.

Winter Sun

In the winter of 1947, Elizabeth and her family set sail for a four-month visit to South Africa. This was Elizabeth and Margaret's first trip abroad and the king hoped it would give Elizabeth a taste of what her role, hopefully in the very distant future, would involve.

The family were greeted in Cape Town by cheering crowds of people. It was hot and sunny, and they were made very welcome. The sisters travelled across the country attending meetings and parties. They went on safari, flew on a plane for the first time in their lives, and saw a glimpse of a world very different to the one they knew at home.

Back home, England was not hot and sunny; in fact it was one of the coldest winters on record. There were power cuts due to fuel shortages. It was so cold people were forced to wear their coats indoors and light their homes with candles. Elizabeth felt very guilty about being away and wanted to show her support.

Three days before she returned to England, Elizabeth turned twenty-one. As part of the celebration she made a speech over the radio that was heard across the world. In her speech, Elizabeth promised to devote her life to the country and the Commonwealth and asked for people to work to bring the world together.

"I DECLARE BEFORE YOU ALL THAT MY WHOLE LIFE, WHETHER IT BE LONG OR SHORT, SHALL BE DEVOTED TO YOUR SERVICE AND THE SERVICE OF OUR GREAT IMPERIAL FAMILY TO WHICH WE ALL BELONG."

Princess Elizabeth, 1947

A Royal Wedding (On a Budget)

King George VI had hoped being away would give Elizabeth the chance to take some time to decide whether she really wanted to marry Philip. Elizabeth did take the time and returned more determined than ever to marry him.

On 9 June 1947, the palace announced that Elizabeth and Philip were engaged to be married. The newspapers went wild with the news. They published stories about the young naval officer explaining his eligibility to marry the future queen. They pointed out that he was a prince himself (of Greece) and a member of the Danish royal family. They reported that he, like Elizabeth, was related to Queen Victoria herself and not only that, but he had also fought bravely in the Second World War.

Most people were excited about the idea of a wedding, but others thought it was in bad taste to be hosting a grand occasion when so many around the country were suffering. Even though the war was over, things had not returned to how they were before.

Elizabeth's father agreed but also felt that as a member of the Royal Family and heir to the throne, the wedding wasn't just about the happy couple. It was a focal point for the nation; a chance for everyone to celebrate a brighter future. The war was over, rationing would one day end, and soon everyone would be able to celebrate in the way they had before the war.

As preparations began, everyone kept in mind that although this was a royal occasion, it was a royal occasion on a ration budget.

RATIONING

During the war, enemy submarines in the Atlantic prevented ships carrying vital supplies, such as food, fuel and cotton, from reaching the United Kingdom. This led to severe shortages which continued long after the war ended. To combat the shortages and to make sure everyone got their share, the British government introduced a system called rationing. During rationing, everyone in the country, including members of the Royal Family, were given a book filled with coupons that allowed them to buy a certain quantity of products such as clothing, meat, sugar or petrol. Rationing began with petrol in 1939 followed by food in January 1940. Clothes began being rationed in 1941 and soap in 1942. Rationing continued on various products until 1954.

Planning the wedding was complicated by rationing, particularly the clothes. In England, the average clothing allowance for an adult was forty-eight coupons, but the government agreed to make allowances for Elizabeth and her family. The wedding was to be filmed and would be seen on newsreels in cinemas across the globe. While it would have been fairer to make everyone stick to their allowance, the government felt that, as representatives of Great Britain, it was important that Elizabeth and her attendants look their best. For this reason, Elizabeth was to be given one hundred coupons for her dress and twenty-three for each of the bridesmaids. Elizabeth's dress was made of ivory silk and tulle, decorated with pearls and crystals and embroidered with flowers.

After the wedding was announced, gifts from well-wishers all over the world flooded in. The presents were displayed in St James's Palace, London and people were able to buy tickets to see them.

The big day took place on 20 November 1947. Elizabeth was driven to Westminster Abbey in the Irish State Coach, with her proud father by her side.

King George was happy for his daughter but a little sad that their cosy family foursome was no more. After the wedding, he sent her a letter saying,

"I CAN, I KNOW, ALWAYS COUNT ON YOU, AND NOW PHILIP, TO HELP US IN OUR WORK. YOUR LEAVING US HAS LEFT A GREAT BLANK IN OUR LIVES BUT DO REMEMBER THAT YOUR OLD HOME IS STILL YOURS."

King George VI, 1947

The wedding was a great success and after the ceremony the family gathered to feast on more than a dozen cakes.

Press Intrusion

The spectacle came at a cost for the couple. People were interested in Elizabeth from the moment she was born, but after the all the attention she got at the wedding, people wanted to know even more about the young newlyweds. Photographers went to extreme lengths to capture shots of the happy couple on their honeymoon, hiding among the trees to get pictures of them on their way to church. But Elizabeth and Philip didn't allow the intrusion to upset them too much; instead they looked forward to the start of their new lives together.

A ROYAL WIFE AND MOTHER

When Elizabeth and Philip returned from honeymoon the couple settled in London. Keen to keep his eldest daughter close by, the king had granted the newlyweds the use of Clarence House, less than a mile away from Buckingham Palace. But they couldn't move in right away. Clarence House needed renovating. While they were waiting they split their time between both Kensington Palace and Buckingham Palace with Elizabeth's mother and father.

This was a happy time for Elizabeth. The couple were very much in love. As heir to the throne, Elizabeth had her royal duties, and Philip had a job at the Admiralty – the government department responsible for the Royal Navy. The couple were busy but they still had a lot of time to spend with one another in the evenings. Philip was sociable and lively and they made lots of fun friends. When in London they went to the theatre, hosted dinners and went to parties. At weekends they could retreat to a country house named Windlesham Moor which they had leased in Sussex.

On 14 November 1948, at Buckingham Palace, Elizabeth gave birth to a baby boy, whom she named Charles Philip Arthur George. Just as when she was born, when the news was reported in the papers, people from all over the world sent gifts of hand-knitted baby clothes, toys and letters of congratulations to celebrate the new prince. The new family received so much mail that Buckingham Palace set up a special department to catalogue the gifts and reply to all the letters.

A Move to Malta

As well as becoming a new father, Philip had other obligations to attend to. He was still enrolled in the navy and though he had taken time away from the ocean to work in London at the Admiralty, he was keen to get back to sea. In 1949, Philip was appointed second in command of a type of ship called a destroyer named HMS *Chequers*. When not sailing around, HMS *Chequers* was stationed in Malta, an island in the Mediterranean. In order to take command, Philip had to move to Malta. Elizabeth and baby Charles moved with him.

In Malta, Elizabeth and Philip lived in an 18th-century home named the Villa Guardamangia, just outside of the capital, Valletta. Growing up in London, all of Elizabeth's trips out had been meticulously planned: she was followed by the press and surrounded by security. In Malta, she was free to go as she pleased. She had a car and drove around the cobbled streets whenever she liked. Rather than being a princess with people watching her every move, in Malta, Elizabeth felt like she was just another navy wife. She was able to go to shops or the hairdresser, spend time with friends and go out for dinner without worrying who was watching them.

Elizabeth returned to England to visit their family often, but Philip was content to be back at sea. On 15 August 1950, the happy family of three became four, when Elizabeth gave birth to a daughter she named Anne Elizabeth Alice Louise at Clarence House, London. Not long after Anne was born, Philip received more good news when he found out he had been promoted to command his very own ship, the HMS *Magpie*.

Elizabeth and Philip returned to Malta as a family of four. Free from the British press they were able to enjoy one another's company and a relatively 'normal' life, though the children often spent time with their grandparents in London.

Queen Elizabeth and Philip with Charles and Anne

Princess Elizabeth Reports for Duty

But this happy time of freedom could not last forever. At home King George VI did not look well. Once youthful and active, he was now tired and pale with a cough that would not go away. Doctors diagnosed the king with a disease called lung cancer and said he needed an operation to get better.

While everyone was sure the king would make a full recovery, he needed time to get well again. Elizabeth knew that she could help. She knew she needed to return to Britain and take on many of his duties.

These duties included greeting foreign dignitaries such as presidents and royalty from all over the world, the Trooping of the Colour and overseas tours to the Commonwealth including a trip to Canada.

Elizabeth was well prepared. Her father had taught her everything he knew. Elizabeth was happy to help her father and the country, but she couldn't do it all by herself. She needed her husband by her side. This meant that Philip had to step down from his command of the HMS *Magpie* and his career in the navy, until the king was better. Both he and Elizabeth hoped it wouldn't be for long.

In 1951, Elizabeth rode in her father's place at the Trooping of the Colour, and she hosted dinners for visiting dignitaries including the King of Norway.

TROOPING THE COLOUR

The Trooping of the Colour is a military parade that takes place every year to mark the sovereign's birthday. The 'colour' refers to flags that represent each of the regiments of the army. Each regiment has a different flag. Traditionally, these flags were used on the battlefield so soldiers could find their regiment easily. For a soldier, being able to find your regiment among the chaos of the battlefield could mean the difference between life and death. To make sure everyone was familiar with their flag (colour), they were paraded (or trooped) in front of everyone in the regiment. Each year a different regiment's colours are chosen.

In October 1951, Elizabeth took the place of her father on a tour of North America and Canada. It was her very first transatlantic flight. Going overseas meant leaving her beloved children behind. Even flying by plane, Canada was sixteen hours away. Thankfully, like her mother and father, Elizabeth and Philip had the help of two nannies, Nurse Lightbody and Mabel Anderson. But it was still hard for her to be away. Anne was just a baby and the tour meant that both Philip and Elizabeth had to miss Charles's third birthday.

In winter 1951, the press reported the king was on the mend. He was able to attend family events again and seemed to be a lot more like his old self. But while he was feeling better, he wasn't quite well enough to set off on a scheduled tour of New Zealand and Australia that had been planned for some time. Rather than cancel the tour, King George and the palace decided that Elizabeth and Philip should go in his place.

Saying Goodbye

On 31 January 1952, Princess Elizabeth and Prince Philip boarded a plane leaving a cold London to fly away on tour. Her father King George VI and Elizabeth, Queen Consort, were at the airport to wave them goodbye.

Flying to Australia non-stop wasn't possible in 1952 and so the journey was broken up into shorter flights, taking in the sights along the way. One of the first stops was Kenya in east Africa. In Kenya, Elizabeth and Philip stayed at a hotel called Treetops. While in Kenya, and on most royal visits, Elizabeth and Philip attended state dinners, but they got the chance to go on safari too.

It started as a fun trip. They saw rhinos,

elephants, antelope and baboons and Elizabeth enjoyed taking photographs of everything they saw.

Rhino

Sad News

Elizabeth and Philip didn't get much time to enjoy their trip, as less than a week after they had left London, Elizabeth's father, King George VI died in his sleep at Sandringham House. He was just fifty-six years old.

Elizabeth and Philip had just returned from watching an elephant with her calves when they heard the news. Elizabeth was devastated and wept. She had known this day would come, but she never thought that it would come so soon. She had had no idea when she boarded the flight from London that it would be the very last time she saw her father. But Elizabeth didn't cry for long. Her father had prepared her for this day from when she was ten years old. Elizabeth knew what her duty was.

As queen, Elizabeth knew she needed to be strong in order to best serve her country, just as her father had done before her, but first she needed to get home. She set to work writing letters of apology to those she would no longer be able to visit on the tour while her secretaries organized her return. Elizabeth's life would never be the same. Her father was gone. She had left England a princess and was returning a queen – Queen Elizabeth II.

A NEW QUEEN

It was a long journey. Storms delayed the plane from taking off, and once in the air it was a twenty-four-hour flight to London. The plane, carrying the new Queen and her husband, landed on 7 February.

If Elizabeth had wanted a quiet return home, she was disappointed. As she stepped off the plane and on to the tarmac she was met by Prime Minister Winston Churchill and the cabinet. They were there to offer their condolences but also their service. As queen, Elizabeth was now the head of state, which meant she had an important role in government. Although she would have to remain neutral regarding political matters, as queen, Elizabeth would be expected to have weekly meetings, called audiences, with the prime minister to keep up to date as to what was going on.

THE PRIME MINISTER AND THE CABINET

In the United Kingdom the head of the government is called the prime minister. Unlike the king or queen, who is the head of state, the prime minister is the leader of the political party voted into power by the people in what is called a general election.

In a general election, people over the age of eighteen are asked to vote for a candidate to represent their region or constituency in the House of Commons. The United Kingdom is divided into 650 constituencies. Each constituency is allowed one seat in the House of Commons. The prime minister is normally the leader of the party whose candidates win the most seats in the House of Commons. Once a political party wins the House, the leader is invited to see the king or queen, who asks them to form a government in his or her name.

To form a government, the prime minister chooses around twenty members of his or her party to make up a group of ministers called the cabinet. The prime minister and the cabinet are in charge of making most of the important decisions in the government. Each member of the cabinet is responsible for a specific government department, such as education, health, transport and foreign affairs.

Hitting the Ground Running

Work began almost the moment Elizabeth walked into Clarence House. There were letters of sympathy to answer, both from the public and from heads of state from all over the world. There were new staff to meet and discuss how they would best serve her. There were portraits to sit for, so that new stamps and coins could be issued with her image and, most importantly of all, there were the red boxes filled with government papers for her to read and sign.

RED BOXES

As queen, Elizabeth is the head of state. As head of state, she receives a red box containing papers from the government every day, including weekends and holidays. The only two days Elizabeth does not receive a box are Easter Sunday and Christmas Day. These papers contain summaries of what the government is doing, and what is happening around the country and the world. These red boxes are delivered to the Queen by a person called the Page of the Presences. The Queen has to read all of the papers contained in the box every day and sign them to show that she has seen and approved what is written.

The next day, on 8 February, Elizabeth was officially proclaimed 'Queen Elizabeth II, by the Grace of God Queen of this Realm and of Her other Realms and Territories, Head of the Commonwealth, Defender of the Faith'.

Elizabeth grew into the role quickly. As a girl, Elizabeth's father had invited her to sit with him and discuss the red boxes he received. He had wanted her to be prepared, and she was. Elizabeth was a quick reader and made useful notes in the margins of the papers, even taking the time to correct spelling errors where she came across them.

As well as office work, there was work outside of home. Elizabeth had already represented her family at openings and sporting events, but this increased dramatically now she was queen. She awarded honours and prizes and held receptions and parties for foreign dignitaries in her home. Her schedule was packed and each moment of her day was accounted for from her morning cup of Earl Grey tea to when she went to bed.

One of the queen's first official duties as monarch was to open Parliament. The State

Opening of Parliament usually took place in May, but the queen's first Opening of Parliament was on 4 November 1952 and was her first state occasion. The State Opening of Parliament marks the beginning of a parliamentary year.

THE STATE OPENING OF PARLIAMENT

For the Opening of Parliament, the Queen travels to the Palace of Westminster in the State coach. Once she arrives the Queen dresses in red velvet robes trimmed with gold lace and lined with black and white fur called ermine, called the Robes of State, before leading a procession into the House of Lords. Once she is seated in the House of Lords, an official, who holds the title of Black Rod, goes to summon the House of Commons.

The door to the House of Commons is slammed in Black Rod's face. This is a symbol of how the

House of Commons is elected by the people and independent from the Queen and the monarchy. Black Rod knocks on the closed door three times, before leading members of the House of Commons to the House of Lords to listen to the Queen read a speech that has been written by the government. The speech sets out the government's plan for the year.

The Queen cannot enter the House of Commons herself. In fact no monarch has set foot in the House of Commons since 1642 when King Charles I stormed into the House of Commons to arrest five members of parliament for treason – an act which led to a civil war.

For Elizabeth's first Opening of Parliament, thousands of people lined the streets to watch as she drove to and from the Palace of Westminster. If Elizabeth had been watched before, it was nothing to her life now. She was the most famous woman in the world. Everything she did and every word she said, unless to her most trusted friends, would be quoted and remembered long afterwards. Elizabeth tried to take it all in her stride and the press remarked on how well being queen seemed to suit her.

Elizabeth's first state occasion went well. She spoke clearly during her speech and she didn't stumble in her robes. Although the speech is written by the government, Elizabeth began her speech with a tribute to her father. The Opening of Parliament was an excellent rehearsal for an even bigger state occasion she was preparing for – her coronation.

BECOMING QUEEN

Elizabeth had attended her father's coronation when she was eleven years old and knew it was an important and solemn occasion. The ceremony itself dated back over 900 years, but Elizabeth's coronation would be a bit different. Elizabeth's coronation would be filmed so people all over the world could witness the moment when she became queen.

A Queen Prepares

With so many people watching, Elizabeth wanted to be ready to make sure she didn't make any mistakes. First Elizabeth wanted to practise what it would be like to walk in her gown. Elizabeth's coronation gown was made of silk and had a train that was more than six metres (nineteen feet) long. Rather than damage the precious silk, Elizabeth rehearsed by walking up and down the ballroom of Buckingham Palace, wearing sheets pinned together. Elizabeth wanted to time her walk perfectly to make sure she would arrive at the altar on time.

As well as her gown, the Queen would be expected to wear the St Edward's Crown that weighed more than 2 kilograms (nearly 5 pounds). Elizabeth practised wearing the crown for long periods of time before the coronation to make sure her neck was strong enough to bear its weight.

THE QUEEN'S CROWNS

St Edward's Crown

The St Edward's Crown was made in 1661 for King Charles II and is similar in design to the original crown that was melted down by Oliver Cromwell. Many believe it to be made of some of the same gold as the original crown which dated back to Edward the Confessor, the last Anglo-Saxon king of England, often

known as St Edward. The St Edward's Crown
is used solely for the coronation and is kept at
Westminster Abbey as it is considered a holy
relic due to its association with St Edward.
The St Edward's Crown weighs over
2.23 kilograms (4.9 pounds).

St Edward's Crown

Imperial State Crown

The Imperial State Crown was made for Queen
Victoria in 1838, but many of the stones
are much older. The crown is topped with a

diamond-encrusted cross with a sapphire in the centre. The sapphire was believed to have been set in a ring worn by Edward the Confessor more than one thousand years ago. The crown also contains teardrop pearls that once belonged to Queen Elizabeth I and a strangely shaped ruby which was worn as a ring by King Henry V at the Battle of Agincourt.

The Imperial State Crown is worn for the State Opening of Parliament as the crown is a symbol of supreme authority.

The coronation ceremony was not short. It was scheduled to last for about three hours, during which all eyes would be on the Queen. Elizabeth knew there would be no opportunities for her to nip to the bathroom. Elizabeth prepared for the big day by eating boiled eggs and lots of salt to make sure she wouldn't need to run to a different throne.

The Big Day

On 2 June 1953, crowds gathered on the rain-soaked streets of London to watch as Elizabeth rode in a golden carriage to Westminster Abbey for the ceremony. Some well-wishers camped out for as long as two days, just for the chance to catch a glimpse of Elizabeth as she passed by. There was an air of excitement as people sang songs in the rain to pass the time. Elizabeth was delighted to see so many people braving the rain to wave flags as she passed, with Philip at her side.

As well as people who had travelled to London, people all over the country prepared to watch. Elizabeth's coronation was the first to be shown on television. When people heard the news that the coronation was going to be shown on television, record numbers rushed out to buy sets so that they could watch Elizabeth be crowned queen.

A Shaky Start

A choir of 400 sang as Elizabeth entered Westminster Abbey. Elizabeth had done everything she could to prepare, but as she attempted to walk down the aisle, she found she couldn't move. Her long train had caught on the carpet. Thinking quickly, Elizabeth asked the Archbishop of Canterbury to give her a push to get her moving. It worked and soon she made it to the altar.

Once at the altar the Queen was surrounded by a canopy and her silk gown was changed for a simple white dress. The canopy hid Elizabeth from the cameras and the congregation as she was anointed with holy oil. Once this was complete, her ladies-in-waiting helped Elizabeth into golden robes.

Once in her robes, the canopy was removed and the archbishop lowered the sparkling crown on to her head, trumpets sounded, and the crowd cried, 'God save the Queen'.

From the front row, Elizabeth's son Charles, aged four, watched as his mother was lifted on to the throne and his father, Prince Philip, knelt and pledged to serve her, with the words, "I, Philip, Duke of Edinburgh, do become your liege man of life and limb, and of earth worship."

While Elizabeth was crowned queen, Philip

did not become king. This is because only men who inherit the throne and are therefore ruling monarchs become king. Instead Philip became Prince Consort.

When Queen Elizabeth and her prince consort left Westminster Abbey, they drove through London back to Buckingham Palace. Rather than go straight there, they took a route which meant as many people as possible got the chance to see the new Queen. Well-wishers lined the streets all along Whitehall and Pall Mall to Piccadilly through Hyde Park and down Oxford Street and Regent Street.

At the palace the Queen sat for official photographs before stepping out on to the balcony with her family. At the end of the day, when all the dignitaries and photographers had gone home, the Queen relaxed into a chair grateful to be on her own at last. But the peace couldn't last long.

The Changing of the Guard

When her father King George VI died, it wasn't just Elizabeth's life that changed. Things changed for her family too. Just as she had had to curtsy before her father, now Charles and Anne had to show her the same honour, and her mother and sister, too. Elizabeth's mother became the Queen Mother instead of Queen Consort and moved from her home in Buckingham Palace to Clarence House.

Elizabeth knew better than anyone how hard the change was going to be for her children. While her father was king, he had always made time for his daughters and Elizabeth did her best to do the same, but it was going to be difficult. Being Queen was more than a full-time job; it was her whole life.

Queen of the World

In November of 1953, Elizabeth and Philip set off again on the tour that was cut short by her father's death. The tour was to last five months and cover 66,000 kilometres (41,000 miles). They visited countries within the Commonwealth such as Jamaica, Australia, New Zealand, Tonga and Uganda. The tour was considered important to maintain a good relationship with these countries, and also for Elizabeth to introduce herself as the new leader of the organization and to some countries as their head of state.

TRAVELLING THE WORLD

A royal tour might look like a long and luxurious holiday to exotic places, but it is far from it. There is very little time for lounging on the beach. When on tour, Elizabeth travels with an estimated 4.5 tonnes of luggage marked in gold with the words 'The Queen'. The Queen also travels with an entourage of 50 members of staff including ladies-in-waiting, secretaries and security officers to help her with her busy schedule.

Queen Elizabeth II is the most well-travelled monarch of all time having visited nearly 120 countries during her reign.

On this Commonwealth tour, Elizabeth made more than 102 speeches and shook countless hands. She travelled with a vast wardrobe of outfits suited to every possible occasion and often had to change multiple times a day. These outfits included her coronation gown which she wore to open Australia's parliament.

Everywhere Elizabeth and Philip went, they were met with crowds of people who wanted to catch a glimpse of the new queen. Not only did the tour involve lots of travel, meeting new people and smiling all the time, it also involved being away from Charles and Anne and her mother over Christmas. It was hard work but it was considered a great success. The countries she visited were pleased to have Elizabeth as their new queen.

Rather than wait for their mother in London, Charles and Anne sailed to meet their mother in Gibraltar on the Royal Yacht *Britannia*. Five months was a long time to be apart, but they had been well looked after, not only by their nannies, but also by the Queen Mother and Princess Margaret who loved spending time with them. If Elizabeth found it hard to be away from her family, she didn't let it show. Her father had taught her it was her duty to serve not only her country but also the Commonwealth and it was a duty she took on willingly.

Royal Yacht Britannia

Back at the palace, Elizabeth's duties continued as before. The government kept her up to date with the red boxes that were delivered every day, but also with a weekly visit with the Prime Minister.

128

AN AUDIENCE WITH THE QUEEN

Even though the Queen is a constitutional monarch and not allowed to make laws, she is still an important part of the government. After a general election, the leader of the winning party is invited to Buckingham Palace for an audience with the Queen. During this meeting, the Queen asks the potential prime minister whether he or she will form a government in her name. The answer is usually yes.

After this initial audience, the prime minister is invited to visit the Queen once a week in her audience room. During the audience the prime minister and the Queen can talk about anything they like in the strictest confidence. And while the Queen is not allowed to attempt to change government policy, she is allowed to express her opinion on what is going on, something which she must avoid doing publicly. No record is kept of what is discussed.

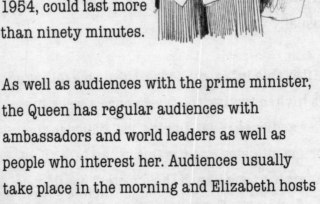

Winston Churchill

An audience with the Queen usually lasts around twenty minutes, but audiences with Sir Winston Churchill, the prime minister in 1954, could last more than ninety minutes.

As well as audiences with the prime minister, the Queen has regular audiences with ambassadors and world leaders as well as people who interest her. Audiences usually take place in the morning and Elizabeth hosts some two to three hundred a year.

A Princess in Love

One of the items discussed in her audience with the prime minister were matters within her own family. As queen, Elizabeth wasn't just head of state and head of the Commonwealth, she was head of her family, which put her in a difficult position regarding her sister. In 1954, Elizabeth's sister Margaret was in love with a man named Group Captain Peter Townsend and wished to marry him, but there was a problem. Peter Townsend had been previously married and was divorced. When plans for the marriage became known to the British government they did not approve. They demanded that in order to marry Peter, Margaret would have to waive her right to succession and her place on something called the 'Civil List', which was her right to an income from the government for her service to the crown. Even if Margaret did this, she would still not be allowed to marry within a church. This was because at the time the Church of England, of which Queen Elizabeth was the head, did not allow divorced people to remarry in church if the person they had been married to were still alive. As queen, many people felt that Elizabeth could change this rule which many thought was outdated and unrealistic, but she did not.

Margaret was broken-hearted, but like Elizabeth, she was her father's daughter and understood the importance of duty and sacrifice. Unlike her uncle, King Edward VIII, Margaret chose her family.

"I WOULD LIKE IT TO BE KNOWN THAT I HAVE DECIDED NOT TO MARRY GROUP CAPTAIN PETER TOWNSEND. I HAVE BEEN AWARE THAT, SUBJECT TO MY RENOUNCING MY RIGHTS OF SUCCESSION, IT MIGHT HAVE BEEN POSSIBLE FOR ME TO CONTRACT A CIVIL MARRIAGE. BUT MINDFUL OF

"THE CHURCH'S TEACHINGS THAT CHRISTIAN MARRIAGE IS INDISSOLUBLE, AND CONSCIOUS OF MY DUTY TO THE COMMONWEALTH, I HAVE RESOLVED TO PUT THESE CONSIDERATIONS BEFORE OTHERS."

Princess Margaret, 1955

This rule did not change until 2002, when the church recognized that while people went into marriage intending to stay together until they died, there were sometimes differences that could not be overcome. They agreed that in special circumstances people could marry within the church if their former partner were still alive.

Margaret's heartbreak didn't last forever. In 1958, Margaret met a photographer called Antony Armstrong-Jones at a friend's dinner party and fell in love. Margaret and Antony married, with the Queen's blessing, in 1960, and sailed away on honeymoon on the Royal Yacht *Britannia*.

A MODERN FAMILY

Elizabeth's children were growing up, but they were growing up in a different world to the one she had grown up. Most upper-class families in the 1950s sent their children to school, rather than educate them at home as she was. In 1956, Prince Charles became the first member of the Royal Family to go to school. Elizabeth and Philip sent Charles, and later Anne, away to boarding school so that their lives would not be as disrupted when their parents were busy or had to go on tour.

Charles went to the same schools his father had attended: Cheam Preparatory School in Berkshire, followed by Gordonstoun in Scotland. Anne was educated at home by a governess until she went to a boarding school called Benenden. Before Anne went to Benenden her mother re-formed the 1st Buckingham Palace Girl Guides, which she and her sister had enjoyed so much growing up.

On 19 February 1960, Buckingham Palace announced the birth of Queen Elizabeth's third child, Prince Andrew Albert Christian Edward. Prince Andrew was the first child to be born to a reigning monarch since Princess Beatrice was born to Queen Victoria in 1857, more than a hundred years before.

Four years later, on 10 March 1964, the royal couple welcomed their fourth and final child into the world, Edward Antony Richard Louis.

Elizabeth was now a mother of four with a full-time international job; she was busy, but some people felt she was out of date. The 1960s were a time of great change – people listened to a new type of music called rock and roll, teenagers stayed out late and didn't always do what their parents said, and people wore daring fashions. Young women wore short skirts called miniskirts and young men grew their hair long. Elizabeth did none of these things. Elizabeth wore clothes similar to the ones she had always worn, the ceremonies she took part in dated back hundreds of years and the music that was played at them was positively medieval.

Some people felt that the Queen was out of touch, not only with her life and fashion, but also with how they wanted her to behave. Elizabeth had always prided herself on being a symbol of strength; she had rarely, if ever, been seen to cry or even be cross. In the world she grew up in, that was what was expected, but now people felt that was cold. They wanted to see how she felt and see that she felt for them when times were hard.

Too Cool in a Crisis?

On 21 October 1966 a disaster shook Great Britain when a heap of waste, left over from a local coal mine, collapsed and engulfed Pantglas Junior School in the Welsh village of Aberfan. The school was almost completely buried and as rescuers rushed to the scene, it became clear that many had been killed.

News of the accident spread quickly. Prince Philip arrived by helicopter within hours of the tragedy where he met rescuers, and people who had lost loved ones.

As the scale of the incident became clear, many people felt that the Queen should have been at the scene to help support people, too. Her brother-in-law, Antony Armstrong-Jones, now Lord Snowdon, was there. Lord Snowdon made cups of tea for people and visited grieving families. Many felt the Queen should have done the same. But the Queen did not come.

One hundred and forty-four people were killed at Aberfan: twenty-eight adults and one hundred and sixteen children. People were angry. They believed Elizabeth lacked sympathy for the people of Aberfan, but that wasn't true. Elizabeth was heartbroken. But Elizabeth didn't think a visit would be in the people's best interest. Whenever the Queen goes anywhere it takes rigorous planning; she needs security and an escort from both her household staff but also local law enforcement. Elizabeth felt that this would be too much of a distraction and could even damage the rescue efforts that were still taking place.

Instead, Elizabeth arrived after the rescue efforts had stopped, eight days after the disaster. For many families in the village this meant that any hope of finding their loved ones alive was gone. While in Aberfan, the Queen met with the tired rescuers and grieving families including a woman who had lost seven members of her family in the disaster. Elizabeth sat with her for more than half an hour to console her. It was the first of many visits the Queen would make to the village after the disaster.

But people felt the Queen's reaction had been too slow. The world was quicker than when she came to the throne. More people had televisions and radios than ever before and were able to find out news quickly; they wanted the Queen to move quickly too. One thing was for certain – something needed to change. People wanted to know who the Queen really was, but how?

The First Reality-TV Star

Elizabeth had allowed the cameras to film her wedding and her coronation, cameras followed her on official visits and tours, but much about her life was still a mystery to people and this was becoming a problem. As head of state, with an income from the government for her work, many people wondered what Elizabeth actually did and whether the monarchy was worth the money that was spent on it. To some, the foreign tours, important for international relations, looked like extended holidays and state banquets looked like an excuse for very rich people to have a good party. With so much ceremony and tradition, the monarchy looked old and out of date.

To change this, one of Elizabeth's advisors suggested she take part in a documentary. They believed that letting cameras into Elizabeth's home and family would give people a chance to see who she really was. The public, her subjects, would see that behind the crown and the palaces she was a busy working mother of a modern family, just like so many others. Long before *Keeping Up With the Kardashians*, *Royal Family* became one of the first reality-television programmes ever made.

Lights, Camera, Action!

The cameras followed Elizabeth and her family for most of 1968, both in public and in private. They joined her on tour and at the family breakfast table. The film followed Prince Charles water-skiing at the beach and Prince Philip flying a plane. The film showed the exciting parts of being queen such as meeting the president of the United States of America as well as the less interesting parts such as spending long hours at her desk answering letters and approving speeches.

Not everybody in the family liked the documentary. They felt that they were entitled to a private life away from the cameras. Elizabeth worried too; she thought that people would find the documentary boring. She had been taught that the monarchy relied on the mystery, so she thought that if people knew what actually went on between the ceremonies and tours and found out that her family was just like any other, they would lose interest and not understand why they were important. She was wrong.

Royal Family aired on 21 June 1969 and was a huge success. The programme attracted more than forty million viewers in the United Kingdom and 400 million more in 130 countries around the world. In the United Kingdom,

Royal Family was repeated five times to give people who hadn't caught it the first time the chance to see the programme everyone was talking about. Rather than boring, people found Elizabeth funny and engaging and could see that she worked very hard.

Looking to the Future

The documentary made people more excited about Elizabeth and her family than ever before. As well as it being a chance to get to know her better, Elizabeth hoped it would be a chance for them to get to know her children better, particularly her eldest son, Charles, who would one day be king.

The documentary aired at just the right time, as a few months later, on 1 July 1969, Charles took part in a special ceremony all of his own at Caernarvon Castle, Wales. The ceremony, called an Investiture, pronounced him Prince of Wales.

During the ceremony, Elizabeth placed a crown on her son's head and an amethyst ring, symbolizing unity with Wales, on his finger.

Charles made the same pledge to his mother as his father had done at her coronation, to be her 'liege man of life and limb', after which, Elizabeth kissed him on the cheek.

Elizabeth hoped the ceremony would show people that Charles was now a man and was not only capable but willing to do his duty to his country when it became time for him to take the throne. This was important to Elizabeth, because she had not been much older than Charles when her own father had died and she became queen. Elizabeth was proud of her son and wanted the country to know, that if the worst did happen, the country and the monarchy would be in good hands. In 1969, no one knew just how long this would be.

Queen in Space

Later that year Elizabeth showed people that she was looking to the future of not only Great Britain and the Commonwealth, but the solar system, too. On 20 July 1969, the world watched as NASA astronaut Neil Armstrong took man's first steps on the Moon. Before he returned to his spacecraft Neil left a gift from the Queen on the Moon's surface. It was a message that read,

"ON BEHALF OF THE BRITISH PEOPLE I SALUTE THE SKILL AND COURAGE WHICH BROUGHT MAN TO THE MOON. MAY THIS INCREASE THE KNOWLEDGE AND WELLBEING OF MANKIND."

Queen Elizabeth II, 1969

When the astronauts returned to Earth, Elizabeth invited them to visit her and her family at Buckingham Palace.

A Historic Walk

Elizabeth may never have set foot on the moon herself, but she did continue her tours of the Commonwealth, and it was on one of these tours that she took a historic walk of her own.

In 1970 Elizabeth went on a tour of Australia and New Zealand with her children, Charles and Anne. With the success of the documentary, Elizabeth knew people wanted to see more of her and to get the chance to meet her. Rather than wave to the crowds from her vehicle as it passed by, Elizabeth walked among them, talking to people as she went and accepting flowers offered to her. Elizabeth enjoyed her 'walkabout' so much, it became a regular part of royal visits for both her and the rest of the Royal Family.

The tour was important for another reason. As well as renewing relationships with members of the Commonwealth, it was an opportunity for Elizabeth to spend some time with her children, just as her father had done when she joined him on their trip to South Africa before her engagement to Philip. Elizabeth knew it wouldn't be long before they married and had children of their own.

A Brave Daughter

In November 1973, Princess Anne became the first of Elizabeth's children to get married. Her husband was a fellow horse rider and Olympic Gold Medallist, Captain Mark Phillips. To mark the occasion, the government announced that their wedding day would be a national holiday. They married in front of 1,500 guests at Westminster Abbey. Newspapers were filled with pictures of the happy day.

Less than a year later, Princess Anne and her husband Mark Phillips were in the news again, for a far less happy reason. On 20 March 1974, the royal couple were on their way to Buckingham Palace in a Rolls Royce when a man stopped the car and attempted to kidnap Princess Anne. The attempt was unsuccessful due to the quick thinking and bravery of Anne's security guard, the police and members of the public present at the time.

The Queen awarded medals to the brave men who saved her daughter, including Ronald Russell, a former boxer who helped capture the attempted kidnapper. For his bravery, Ronald was awarded the George Medal, the highest honour available to civilians. When Elizabeth presented the award she said, "The medal is from the Queen of England; the thank you is from Anne's mother."

A Silver Celebration

In 1977 Elizabeth celebrated her Silver Jubilee, marking twenty-five years since she became queen. It was a busy year for Elizabeth. As part of the celebrations, she went on tour not only around the United Kingdom, visiting towns and cities, but also Australia, New Zealand, islands in the Pacific, the Caribbean and Canada.

The government declared 7 June 1977 a national holiday, and an estimated one million people travelled to London to watch as Elizabeth rode through the city in a golden coach to a Thanksgiving Service at St Paul's Cathedral. People around the country hung out bunting and made piles of sandwiches to serve at street parties organized to honour the queen's reign.

At the end of the day, Elizabeth lit a bonfire outside Windsor Castle which was the first in a series of bonfires around lit around the United Kingdom and the world.

Elizabeth was touched by just how many people came to see her on each of her visits and organized parties celebrating her reign.

Elizabeth Becomes a Grandmother

Elizabeth was given another reason to celebrate on 15 November 1977 when her daughter, Anne, gave birth to a son, Peter. Peter made Elizabeth a grandmother for the first time. At fifth in line to the throne, it was unlikely that Peter would ever be king and for this reason Anne turned down any sort of title for her little boy. Elizabeth supported her daughter's decision to give her children a more normal life away from the cameras. But even though Peter would not be raised as a little prince he was still very close to his grandmother.

A Dangerous Job

When people see pictures or film of the Queen in her bright hats and coats, smiling and shaking hands with people it is hard to understand why anyone would wish to do her harm. But the

Queen isn't just a smiling lady, she is a head of state: a powerful symbol of Great Britain and its government. Elizabeth's Silver Jubilee had shown her how popular she and her family were. But she was wasn't popular with everyone. In fact, as queen, people who disagree with the actions of Great Britain both at home and abroad see her as a target.

A visit from the Queen is often shrouded in secrecy to prevent anyone who would wish to do her harm from having the time to plan their attack. She is surrounded by security and often has a police escort both to and from where she is going. Her family is given protection from security, too, even more since Anne's attempted kidnap. One place Elizabeth was given extra security was on her visit to Northern Ireland in 1977, when a group called the Irish Republican Army (IRA) made threats against her life. Threats from the IRA were not to be taken lightly as they had claimed responsibility for attacks on cities around Great Britain.

THE TROUBLES AND NORTHERN IRELAND

'The Troubles' refers to the violent conflict that took place in the late 1960s to the late 1990s between Protestant people and Catholic people in Northern Ireland.

In 1921, following the Irish war of Independence, the British government granted twenty-six southern counties of Ireland independence from British rule. They became the Republic of Ireland and most of the people who lived there were Catholic. The British government decided that six counties in the north, where people were mostly Protestant, were to remain part of the United Kingdom. Most of the Protestant people living in Northern Ireland wanted to remain part of the United Kingdom. Many Catholic people living in Northern Ireland, called Nationalists, did not and they faced discrimination and attacks. The Catholic Nationalists believed they could only end the discrimination and attacks by continuing their fight for a united Ireland. Some Nationalists went further and joined a group called the Irish Republican Army or IRA. The IRA hoped that by using armed force and terror tactics both in Northern Ireland and on the British mainland they could bring an end to British rule in Ireland. These terror tactics included bombing civilian and military targets and attacking people with power and influence such as the Prime Minister and the Queen and her family, such as Lord Louis Mountbatten. The conflict between these groups continues to this day.

On 27 August 1979, Lord Louis Mountbatten – Prince Philip's uncle and Elizabeth's second cousin once removed – was killed by a bomb hidden on his boat, in County Sligo, Ireland. His grandson and a member of the crew were also killed in the attack. A group called the Provisional IRA claimed responsibility for the blast. Mountbatten was an important member of the Royal Family. He was a mentor to Prince Charles and Prince Philip and his death hit the family very hard. The attack also underlined how important the need for security was and the threat posed by groups such as the IRA.

The Queen isn't just in danger from terrorist groups, she is also under threat from people who want to attack her because she is so famous. These people hope that by hurting her they can become famous themselves.

On 13 June 1981, Elizabeth was riding her faithful horse, Burmese, during the annual Trooping of the Colour celebration (see page 105) when a man with a gun emerged from the gathered crowd and opened fire. Elizabeth was not hurt in the attack. She steadied her startled horse as the shooter was wrestled to the ground by police and arrested. Thankfully the bullets fired were blanks.

A GROWING FAMILY

While one of Elizabeth's children, Anne, seemed to be happily married and beginning a new family, her eldest son Charles seemed in no hurry to settle down. Journalists filled newspapers with stories speculating as to who the prince might be dating and who he would choose to marry. Elizabeth was anxious to know too, for whoever Charles chose to be his wife would also be his future queen and mother to the future kings and queens of Great Britain. Elizabeth knew Charles needed to choose wisely as she remembered what happened when her uncle, Edward VIII, did not.

It was an important decision, and the prince took his time and advice from members of his family. Eventually, in 1981, Charles proposed to a woman named Lady Diana Spencer. Diana was young and pretty and was from a noble family. Elizabeth and the government approved of his choice. The nation went wild at the news: the handsome prince had met his bride.

Charles and Diana married on 29 July 1981 at St Paul's Cathedral. Diana wore an ivory satin gown with a train measuring seven metres (twenty-three feet) long. More than 600,000 people travelled to London to celebrate alongside the happy couple and an estimated 750 million viewers around the world watched the ceremony on television.

Princess Diana

It was a magical occasion and a great day for Elizabeth as it proved to her that the nation and the world had taken her family to their hearts, just as they had her father's. Elizabeth hoped that Charles and Diana would be as happy as she and Philip were and that with luck, they would soon welcome a new heir to the throne.

They did not have to wait long. On 21 June 1982, Charles and Diana welcomed their first child, Prince William Arthur Philip Louis, into the world. As Charles's first-born son, William was second in line to the throne. Two years later, Charles and Diana welcomed a second son into their family, Henry Charles Albert David.

Charles having two sons meant that Elizabeth's second son, Andrew, moved from second in line to the throne to fourth, but Andrew had other things in mind for his future.

A Prince Goes to War

As head of the armed forces Elizabeth is the only person with the power to declare war. Thankfully Elizabeth never had to do so. The last monarch to declare war was her father King George VI in 1939. As well as being head of the armed forces, Elizabeth also holds a number of other honorary ranks within the military.

All recruits into the armed forces have to pledge their allegiance to the queen. In 1979, Elizabeth's third child, Prince Andrew, took the pledge when he joined the Royal Navy after leaving school. Once in the navy, Andrew trained to become a helicopter pilot. In 1982, like many mothers around the country, Elizabeth watched and worried as her son went to war.

THE FALKLANDS WAR

On 2 April 1982, forces from Argentina in South America invaded islands in the southern Atlantic known as the Falkland Islands. The Falkland Islands had been under British rule for many years, but the Argentinian government believed the islands, which they called Las Islas Malvinas, should belong to Argentina.

To protect the islands, the British government sent thirty warships and 6,000 soldiers to fight the Argentinian forces. Prince Andrew sailed with the HMS *Invincible*. At the beginning of the conflict, the British government suggested Andrew be moved to a safer job within the Royal Navy, but just as her father had when she served with the ATS, Elizabeth insisted Andrew not be given any special treatment, Andrew flew a number of missions as co-pilot on a Sea King helicopter. After two months of fierce fighting, Argentina found that they were outnumbered. The Argentinian government surrendered on 14 June 1982. More than 900 servicemen and women were killed in the conflict. Andrew sailed back to the United Kingdom unharmed. Elizabeth and Philip joined the families of the rest of the crew of HMS *Invincible* to meet them in Portsmouth, UK when they returned home.

Sea King helicopter

With Andrew safe at home, Elizabeth probably thought she could rest easy. With all the security surrounding her what could she possibly have to worry about?

An Intruder Wakes the Queen

On the morning of 9 July 1982, Elizabeth woke up in her bedroom in Buckingham Palace to find a man she did not know sitting in her room. Elizabeth sounded the alarm by pressing a button next to her bed, but no one came. Elizabeth didn't panic; instead she spoke to the man. The man told her how he had climbed into the palace through an open window and asked if he could have a cigarette. He talked to Elizabeth about his problems as she went to look for a cigarette for him and summoned help from another room. When the police finally arrived, the man was arrested.

When questioned, the man confessed that it was not the first time he had broken into Buckingham Palace. Elizabeth's staff were horrified and embarrassed that even though Buckingham Palace was surrounded by police and soldiers, someone was able to break in and get so close to the Queen, not once but twice. Everyone was thankful that the situation wasn't much worse, but the queen's security was increased to make sure it never happened again.

A Year for Celebration

In April 1986 Elizabeth celebrated her sixtieth birthday. Her day began at Windsor Castle where she was woken by a piper playing 'Happy Birthday' on the bagpipes. In the afternoon the Queen appeared on the balcony of Buckingham Palace to be greeted by a crowd of children from all over

Great Britain and the Commonwealth waving daffodils. The children had travelled to London to sing for her birthday and give her flowers.

Next to her on the balcony stood her husband Philip, son Andrew, and Andrew's new fiancée, Sarah Ferguson.

It was a happy day and in the evening the family attended a special birthday concert at the Royal Albert Hall.

Andrew and Sarah married on the 23 July 1986 at Westminster Abbey. It was a beautiful ceremony and Elizabeth was delighted to be surrounded by her whole family: her four children, three now married, and her four grandchildren. After the wedding Elizabeth gave Andrew and Sarah the titles of the Duke and Duchess of York which meant they would be able to help with royal duties. Andrew and Sarah spent their honeymoon on the Royal Yacht *Britannia*. Elizabeth was pleased with the match. Elizabeth hoped Andrew and Sarah would be very happy together – sadly they were not, and in this they were not alone.

A HORRIBLE YEAR

The year 1992 should have been a glorious year of celebration for Elizabeth. It was the year she would celebrate her Ruby Jubilee marking forty years on the throne, but instead it turned into a year she wished she could forget. A year that would end in flames.

As queen, Elizabeth believed that she had a duty to be a symbol of strength and continuity to the country. Her father had taught her that although her life was one of duty it was also a life of great privilege and so she was not allowed to complain.

Elizabeth had married the man of her dreams when she was just twenty-one years old. She had performed her royal duties tirelessly without uttering a word of complaint to the press. Philip had done his duty too, and though he may have complained behind closed doors about having to give up his naval career to follow Elizabeth around the world, he never showed any sign of it. They may have argued and experienced troubles in their marriage, but to the outside world they were a symbol of commitment and love.

The same could not be said for their children. In 1992, it became clear that the marriages of not one but three of her children were falling apart. Media interest in the Royal Family was as high as ever, but instead of glossy, feature-length articles on their work for charity or representing Great Britain abroad, newspapers and magazines were filled with something Elizabeth had done everything in her power to avoid – scandal.

On 19 March 1992, Buckingham Palace announced the separation of the Duke and Duchess of York, Andrew and Sarah. The announcement was closely followed by the news that her daughter Princess Anne was also to separate from her husband Captain Mark Philips.

Elizabeth was sad about the news, both for her children and because she was worried about the scandalous stories in the papers. But even more difficult news was to follow later that year, when the newspapers announced that

Diana, Princess of Wales had granted interviews to a journalist who had written a book. In her interviews Diana confessed how unhappy she had been in her marriage to Elizabeth's eldest son and the heir to the throne, Prince Charles. The couple separated soon after. When the book was released newspapers went wild with the story, some journalists questioning whether a family with so much scandal had any right to lead the country. The Queen despite her wealth and privilege was powerless to stop it.

Great Britain in the 1990s

The year wasn't just hard for the Royal Family, it was hard for many in Great Britain, too. After business booming in the 1980s, the 1990s saw the beginning of a recession. A recession is something that happens when businesses aren't able to make as much money as they used to therefore aren't able to pay as many people to work for them. Lots of people lost their jobs. Without work, people struggled to pay back loans and pay their bills. Many people lost their homes.

With so many people in need, the British government looked for ways to save money. Elizabeth was one of the people they looked to. As queen, Elizabeth had been exempt from paying many taxes, but she agreed to change this, by paying taxes on her income and covering many of her own expenses. This meant that she would cost the government less money and they would have more money to spend on things people in the country needed such as roads, schools and healthcare.

A Fire at the Fortress

With three of her children's marriages in tatters, 1992 been a year of chaos for Elizabeth. It turned out to be a year that would end in flames.

At 11.30 a.m. on 20 November 1992, a fire broke out in the queen's private chapel at Windsor Castle. The blaze spread quickly, engulfing Brunswick Tower, a banqueting hall, and private apartments in the east wing of the castle.

Staff tried to rescue precious items from the burning castle. Elizabeth arrived as fire crews attempted to quench the fire. More than 225 fireman fought the blaze which took twelve hours and 1.5 million gallons of water to put out.

One fifth of the castle was severely damaged or completely destroyed. Experts estimated that it would cost £36.5 million to restore. Like many grand houses, Windsor Castle was not insured because it was so valuable and contained so many priceless works of art.

Even though Windsor Castle was owned by the state, the government weren't sure they wanted to pay the bill. After a year of royal scandal, many members of Parliament didn't think that it was right for the government to pay for the damages. They thought Elizabeth and her family should pay for it themselves.

In order to cover the cost of the damage, Elizabeth agreed to open the castle and its grounds to the public. The palace hoped that the entrance fee would contribute to the repairs.

In her Christmas message Elizabeth said, "1992 is not a year on which I shall look back with undiluted pleasure. In the words of one of my more sympathetic correspondents, it has turned out to be an *annus horribilis*", which is Latin for 'horrible year'.

The damage to Windsor Castle took more than five years to fix – however the marriages of Elizabeth's children were beyond repair.

Windsor Castle

A Fatal Crash

After a difficult separation, Prince Charles and Diana, Princess of Wales finally divorced in 1996. Many hoped it would give them a chance to move on with their lives, but sadly that was not the case.

Diana, while no longer married to Prince Charles, was still a very popular member of the Royal Family. People loved her sense of style, and that she was a loving mother to William and Harry. People also admired the compassion she showed in her work for charity.

On 31 August 1997, one year after their divorce became official, Diana, Princess of Wales, mother of Princes William and Harry, died in a car accident in Paris.

The news was a great shock to everyone in the United Kingdom, some of whom felt the loss as deeply as if they had known Diana.

People looked to Buckingham Palace and Elizabeth for guidance of how to deal with their sadness. But the Queen was not there. Elizabeth was at Balmoral with her family, just as she was every summer. As Charles and Diana were divorced, Elizabeth did not see the need to travel back to London. Elizabeth felt it was her job to look after her grandchildren, who had just lost their mother.

BALMORAL CASTLE

Queen Elizabeth spends her summers in Scotland at a place called Balmoral Castle. The Balmoral Estate was bought as a present by her great-great-grandfather Prince Albert, for his wife Queen Victoria in 1852 and has been a traditional summer home for the Royal Family ever since.

The whole family is invited. At Balmoral, Elizabeth gets to relax and live a more normal life. She even does the washing-up! Traditional activities at Balmoral include riding, walking, hunting, hosting Scottish reels, picnics and barbeques and attending the Highland Games.

Balmoral Castle

"IT'S THE MOST BEAUTIFUL PLACE ON EARTH," SHE SAID. "I THINK GRANNY IS THE MOST HAPPY THERE. I THINK SHE REALLY, REALLY LOVES THE HIGHLANDS... WALKS, PICNICS, DOGS — A LOT OF DOGS, THERE'S ALWAYS DOGS! AND PEOPLE COMING IN AND OUT ALL THE TIME."

Princess Eugenie, 2021

Many people disagreed, they were angry with Elizabeth and felt that as queen and Diana's former mother-in-law, she should help to guide them in their grief. Thousands of people brought flowers to Kensington Palace, and all over the country many thousands more signed books of condolence.

Prime Minister Tony Blair advised Elizabeth to come and meet the people. Elizabeth listened and travelled down from Balmoral to meet with mourners outside Buckingham Palace and lay flowers.

Diana's funeral took place at Westminster Abbey and was watched by millions of people all over the world. After the

Tony Blair

funeral, her body was laid to rest on an island in a lake at her childhood home.

THE NEW MILLENNIUM

Elizabeth celebrated the new year, and the beginning of a new millennium at the Millennium Dome (now known as the O2 Arena) in London, singing 'Auld Lang Syne' and holding hands with her husband Philip and Prime Minister Tony Blair.

In the Christmas Broadcast of 1999, Elizabeth took the opportunity to look back on the last thousand years and some of the changes the world had seen during that time. She also looked back on the changes she had seen during her reign and how different her and her mother's childhoods were from those of her grandchildren.

When Elizabeth was born, only about one third of British homes had electricity, no one had a television in their home and there was no such thing as a home computer. In 1926, only wealthy families had a telephone in their home, but by the year 2000 almost all homes had a telephone and many people had mobile telephones, though they were nowhere near as 'smart' as the ones we have today.

Elizabeth urged people to look towards the future with excitement, but not to let the new technology and developments make them forget about their shared history and caring for one another.

THE CHRISTMAS BROADCAST

The very first Christmas Broadcast was delivered by Elizabeth's grandfather in 1932, six years after she was born. It was transmitted live over wireless radio from Sandringham House to radio sets around Great Britain as well as India, Australia, Canada, Kenya and South Africa.

Elizabeth's father, George VI, continued the tradition of the Christmas Broadcast. But they didn't happen every year until the Second

World War, when George VI used his Christmas message to reassure people and boost morale.

Elizabeth sat at the same desk her father and grandfather used when she made her first Christmas Broadcast over the radio in 1952. In this broadcast, Elizabeth pledged to continue her father's work and asked people to wish her luck for her coronation that was to take place the following year. After her first broadcast, Elizabeth went on to make a broadcast every single year apart from 1969, when her documentary aired instead.

Elizabeth's first televised Christmas Broadcast took place in 1957 and was filmed live. Today Elizabeth records her broadcasts in advance so that they can be played at a convenient local time in countries around the Commonwealth. In 2012, Elizabeth's Christmas message was broadcast for the first time in 3D.

Elizabeth sees her Christmas message as her chance to address the nation and the Commonwealth of Nations from her heart. In it, she is able to express her views about the events she has seen over the previous year and thank people for their service and support.

Elizabeth had seen many changes during her reign both at home and abroad and Elizabeth was sure that the future held many more.

"AND AS I LOOK TO THE FUTURE I HAVE NO DOUBT AT ALL THAT THE ONE CERTAINTY IS CHANGE - AND THE PACE OF THAT CHANGE WILL ONLY SEEM TO INCREASE."

Queen Elizabeth II, 1999

Elizabeth was excited to see what changes lay ahead, both for her, the country and the Commonwealth. Elizabeth had a lot to look forward to.

A Golden Reign

In 2002, Queen Elizabeth celebrated her Golden Jubilee, marking fifty years since she came to the throne. Even though Elizabeth was by now seventy-six years old, ten years past the United Kingdom's age of retirement, she showed no sign of slowing down. Elizabeth knew from when she was a little girl that the job of queen was a job for life. She had pledged to devote her life to serving her country and the Commonwealth and the Golden Jubilee was people's chance to thank her for her fifty years of service.

People all over the globe held parties to celebrate, including British scientists stationed in Antarctica, who held their own 'street party' in temperatures of minus 20°C (68°F). They even played a cricket match on the ice. Elizabeth's chef created a new recipe called

'Jubilee chicken' for people to make for and enjoy at their parties.

To celebrate her Jubilee, Elizabeth travelled to Jamaica, New Zealand, Australia and Canada as well as more than seventy towns and cities around the UK. Elizabeth even visited the sets of soap operas, such as *Emmerdale*, which aired special episodes to celebrate her reign.

As well as visiting people around the country, the Queen celebrated by inviting people into her home, or at least the grounds of her home, by hosting 'Party at the Palace' – a pop concert held in the grounds of Buckingham Palace.

While jubilees were cause for celebration, they were also a cause of sadness for Elizabeth, because the day she inherited the throne was also the day she lost her father. The day a monarch accedes to the throne is called accession day. To mark this day, Elizabeth decided that she would prefer to spend time with her family and people who knew her father well and as she grew older, these people became harder to find.

Saying Goodbye

On the 9 February 2002, the Palace announced that Elizabeth's sister, Princess Margaret, had died peacefully in her sleep aged just seventy-one. Margaret was Elizabeth's best friend and companion from when she was born. Princess Margaret had been ill for some time, but Elizabeth had hoped she would get better. Margaret and Elizabeth had lived through so much together, but having survived two strokes Margaret was unable to survive her third. Margaret's funeral was held on 15 February 2002, fifty years to the day of her father, King George VI.

It was a hard loss for Elizabeth, but it would not be the only loss she felt that year. At 101 years old, Elizabeth's mother's health was failing too. The Queen Mother had become increasingly frail and had developed a cough.

Elizabeth was out riding at Windsor when she was told her mother was feeling unwell. Elizabeth rushed to be at her side. The Queen Mother died at Royal Lodge on 30 March 2002, with Elizabeth at her side. Elizabeth was very close to her mother, speaking to her every day and writing to her whenever she was overseas.

A Fitting Farewell

Elizabeth and palace staff worried that the Queen Mother, who had been ill for some time, may have been forgotten by people and that few would come to her funeral. They were wrong. Hundreds of thousands of people travelled to London to say goodbye. The Queen Mother's coffin was brought to Westminster Hall which was opened to the public so people could pass by and say their farewells. The hall had to be kept open twenty-four hours a day to give the one million people who came the chance to pay their respects.

Elizabeth was touched and overwhelmed. The day before the funeral, Elizabeth made a statement to thank people for the love they had shown her mother and for the support they gave to her and her family.

"I HAVE BEEN DEEPLY MOVED BY THE OUTPOURING OF AFFECTION WHICH HAS ACCOMPANIED HER DEATH."

Queen Elizabeth II, 2002

The Queen Mother's funeral was held at Westminster Abbey where she was laid to rest with her husband George VI and her daughter Margaret.

In just six weeks, the Queen had lost her two closest friends and companions – the two people who had known her since she was a little princess and whom she had spoken to almost every day of her life. Elizabeth was devastated, but just as she had after the death of her father, fifty years before, Elizabeth found the strength to go on.

Elizabeth didn't have to go on alone; as well as her husband Philip, Elizabeth had her children and grandchildren to comfort her. She also had her beloved corgis, including her mother's corgis, who Elizabeth took in and looked after alongside her own.

Second Time Lucky

On 9 April 2005, Elizabeth's eldest son Charles married a woman named Camilla Parker Bowles at a civil ceremony at Guildhall in Windsor. Both Charles and Camilla had been married before and while Charles's ex-wife, Diana, died in 1997, Camilla's ex-husband, Andrew Parker Bowles was still alive. Charles had known Camilla for many years and the couple were very much in love. The wedding marked both Charles and Camilla's second marriage and a historic marriage for the Royal Family as, even though Charles was marrying someone who was divorced, he was allowed to keep his title and place in line to the throne, something that was denied both his aunt, Princess Margaret, and his great-uncle, Edward VIII. Charles was able to marry Camilla due to a change in church law in 2002 (see page 47). Elizabeth attended a blessing ceremony for Charles and Camilla's marriage at St George's

Chapel, Windsor Castle. The celebration was not as big as those for previous royal weddings but Elizabeth hoped the marriage would be much happier. After marrying Charles, Camilla became a member of the Royal Family and took on some of the roles and responsibilities that went with it. Once of these responsibilities was to become a patron for charities.

Camilla Parker Bowles

Standing for What They Believe In

A patron is a person who provides support for a charitable organization either by working with them to raise money and awareness or by donating money to the cause. As patrons, Royal Family members are expected to host and attend events for the charity, make speeches on their behalf and raise awareness of what the charity is trying to achieve. Having a member of the Royal Family as a patron can draw much-needed attention to charities and help them to do their work.

As queen, Elizabeth has been the patron for hundreds of charities during her reign including Cancer Research UK, Girl Guiding and the Royal Society of the Prevention of Cruelty to Animals. Queen Elizabeth is the patron of charities and organizations from all over the world and has worked hard to serve them throughout her life, but there were always far more charities than she was able to manage by herself, especially as she got older. This is where her family were able to step in. Members of the Royal Family are able to choose which charities they would like to work with. Prince Philip was patron and president of many charities and organizations involved in everything from science to the welfare of young people, such as the Duke of Edinburgh's Award (DofE). He was passionate about spending time in nature which was why he chose to become president of the World Wildlife Fund. Elizabeth and Philip's children and grandchildren have continued this tradition. William, Duke of Cambridge, a fan of the arts, became the patron of the British Academy of Film and Television Arts (BAFTA) as well as doing important work raising awareness for a number of mental health charities including one called Heads Together, which he set up with his wife the Duchess of Cambridge with the support of the Royal Foundation.

A Queen in Good Times and Bad

As queen, Elizabeth is expected to be a focal point for people in times of celebration as well as times of tragedy. In July 2005, Elizabeth joined the nation as it held its breath awaiting the decision of the International Olympics committee as to which country would host the 2012 Olympic Games. Many people up and down the country had worked hard preparing the bid, doing everything they could to prove that London would be the best place to host the games. Many felt it was especially important to win the 2012 Olympic games because it would be held in the year of Elizabeth's Diamond Jubilee, celebrating sixty years on the throne.

Crowds gathered in London to await the announcement. Prime Minister Tony Blair said he had been too nervous to watch. Just before 1 p.m. the president of the International Olympics committee announced that Great Britain would host the 2012 Olympic Games. The crowds gathered around the country to hear the announcement went wild. The Red Arrows streaked across the sky over Trafalgar Square leaving a trail of red, white and blue smoke.

Elizabeth was delighted. The last Olympic Games to be held in the United Kingdom took place in 1948 and were opened by her father; she was keen to be able to do the same. Elizabeth released a statement congratulating the delegates for their hard work.

"IT'S A REALLY OUTSTANDING ACHIEVEMENT TO BEAT SUCH A HIGHLY COMPETITIVE FIELD."

Queen Elizabeth II, 2005

Little did Elizabeth know she would have to deliver a different statement the very next day and that the sky across London would be filled with a very different smoke.

7 July Bombings

The day after the celebration, four men carrying explosive devices boarded trains on the London Underground. At 8.50 a.m., three of these men detonated their devices, killing themselves, and killing and injuring many people around them. An hour later, a fourth man detonated his device on board a bus in Tavistock Square. It was a terrorist attack in which a total of fifty-two people were killed and more than seven hundred people were injured.

"I KNOW I SPEAK FOR THE WHOLE NATION IN EXPRESSING MY SYMPATHY TO ALL THOSE AFFECTED AND THE RELATIVES OF THE KILLED AND INJURED. I HAVE NOTHING BUT ADMIRATION FOR THE EMERGENCY SERVICES AS THEY GO ABOUT THEIR WORK."

Queen Elizabeth II, 2005

Elizabeth visited victims of the attack in hospital and donated money to help with their recovery. After the attack, security around the country was increased, particularly around the Royal Palaces and places that the authorities believed may be targeted.

Birthday Twins

In April 2006, Elizabeth celebrated her eightieth birthday by inviting ninety-nine people from around the Commonwealth who were born on the same day to celebrate with her. In a speech Elizabeth called her guests her 'exact twins'. Elizabeth's twins were treated to lunch at Buckingham Palace served on solid silver plates. Her guests were touched and honoured to have been invited. A man named John Forrester, who had travelled from Australia, said that Elizabeth was the "most natural person in the world" who could "endear herself to anybody and everybody".

Dining in such grand surroundings was normal for Elizabeth, but not for many of her guests. Elizabeth put them at their ease by celebrating what they all had in common.

"I DOUBT WHETHER ANY OF US WOULD SAY THE LAST EIGHTY YEARS HAS BEEN PLAIN

SAILING. BUT WE CAN GIVE THANKS FOR OUR HEALTH AND HAPPINESS, THE SUPPORT WE RECEIVE FROM OUR FAMILIES AND FRIENDS."

Queen Elizabeth II, 2006

Help is at Hand

Elizabeth relied on the support of her family a great deal. While in excellent health, at eighty years old Elizabeth wasn't able to perform as many commitments as she had when she was younger so thankfully her children and grandchildren were able to step in.

Elizabeth was a devoted grandmother. Over the years, Elizabeth's grandchildren had been invited to spend holidays with her at Balmoral and Sandringham and she had enjoyed watching them grow up. Elizabeth took a special interest in her eldest grandson, William. As second in line to the throne, Elizabeth felt it was important for him to see what becoming king would mean when the time came. When William attended school, Elizabeth invited him to visit her at weekends. William enjoyed these visits. To William, Elizabeth was just his grandmother who made sure to have his favourite chocolate biscuit cake ready for him when he came for tea.

SANDRINGHAM HOUSE

Sandringham House in Norfolk was bought by Elizabeth's great-grandfather, King Edward VII in 1862. Sandringham is located about 100 miles (161 km) from London and has a working farm on the estate. Sandringham is a special place for Elizabeth as her father, George VI was born and died there. Sandringham is also the home of the Royal Stud where Elizabeth can explore her passion for horse racing, by looking after and breeding some of the world's fastest horses. Elizabeth travels to Sandringham by train.

Elizabeth spends around two months at Sandringham most winters, and hosts Christmas for her children, grandchildren and now great-grandchildren there every year.

Christmas is a lively time for Elizabeth and her family. Her grandchildren like to play pick-up games of football in the grounds and inside there are lots of games of charades to keep everyone entertained. The family exchanges gifts on Christmas Eve. On Christmas morning, Elizabeth and her family go to church on the estate.

On 29 April 2011, William married Catherine Middleton, a woman he had met and fell in love with while at university in Scotland. Like Elizabeth's wedding in 1947, people from all over the country travelled to celebrate with the couple, and millions all over the world watched the ceremony on television. As part of the celebration,

William asked that a tier of his wedding cake be
the chocolate cake his grandmother always served
him when he visited her.

Kate Middleton
and William

Sixty Years of Fun and Games

In 2012, Elizabeth celebrated yet another anniversary, her Diamond Jubilee, marking sixty years since she had ascended to the throne. As with her Silver and Golden Jubilees, it promised to be a year packed with parades, parties, visits and dinners, but that wasn't all. As well as it being an important year for Elizabeth, the year 2012 was an exciting year for Great Britain too, as it was the year of the London Olympic Games.

Having served sixty years on the throne, Elizabeth knew how important it was to make a grand entrance. At the London Olympic Games, Elizabeth made an entrance nobody was ever likely to forget. Elizabeth got a chance to show off her sense of humour, too. During the Opening Ceremony big screens in the arena showed a short film, shot before the games, of Elizabeth's journey to the stadium. In the film, Elizabeth is collected from Buckingham Palace by none other than the famous fictional spy, James Bond, played by actor Daniel Craig. Together Elizabeth and Bond fly through

London by helicopter to the stadium. At the stadium, a real helicopter hovered overhead as someone, who looked just like Elizabeth, in the same pale pink embroidered gown, jumped out and parachuted to the ground. Moments later the commentator announced Elizabeth's arrival. The crowd gasped, could it really be the Queen that jumped out of the helicopter? It was not – it was a stunt performer, but people loved it just the same, especially because it was a side of Elizabeth many people hadn't seen before.

A Great-Grandmother

The following year, Elizabeth's grandson, William and his wife Catherine had a little boy. The happy couple named their son after Elizabeth's father King George VI. William's son, George Alexander Louis, born 22 July 2013, became the third in line to the throne.

Elizabeth had been a great-grandmother since 2010 when Princess Anne's eldest son, Peter, had a little girl he named Savannah. Elizabeth shows how special her great-grandchildren are to her by always leaving special gifts for them in their rooms whenever they come to stay with her. As George grew up, and started saying his first words, he found he was unable to pronounce great-grandmother, or grandmother, so he called Elizabeth 'Gangan' – a name which stuck.

Prince George

THE LONGEST
REIGNING MONARCH

On 9 September 2015, Elizabeth became the United Kingdom's longest reigning monarch, breaking the record previously held by her great-great-grandmother Queen Victoria who reigned for 63 years and 216 days.

Elizabeth said she had never aspired to pass this milestone, and indeed, she had only reigned so long, because her father had died when she was so young.

"INEVITABLY, A LONG LIFE CAN PASS BY MANY MILESTONES. MY OWN IS NO EXCEPTION."

Queen Elizabeth II, 2015

On 10 June 2016, Elizabeth celebrated her ninetieth birthday. While most people retire from their careers long before they reach the age of ninety, the role of queen is a job unlike any other. From the moment her father became king, Elizabeth's career had been decided for her. When her father died Elizabeth took up her role of queen as her duty, and she believed it was her duty to fulfil that role for the rest of her life.

To celebrate her official birthday in June, Elizabeth hosted an enormous street party in front of Buckingham Palace. Elizabeth invited over 10,000 guests including people who worked with the 600 charities and organizations she was associated with. Elizabeth used the occasion to thank people for all their hard work serving the community and to raise money for the charities she supported. Elizabeth rode through the streets of London in an open-topped car wearing a bright pink coat as thousands of people cheered and congratulated her. Waving beside her, as always on occasions such as these, was Prince Philip who had turned ninety-five just two days before. As they drove through the streets passing thousands of people wishing her a happy birthday, Elizabeth knew they were cheering for him too, because they were a team.

Prince Philip Retires

From Elizabeth's first days as queen, Philip had been there to support her in her work. As a young queen, Elizabeth often felt shy on public engagements and sometimes at a loss for what to say. Philip always knew when to step in if she was overwhelmed and how to break the ice if she felt awkward.

At a party celebrating their fiftieth wedding anniversary in 1997 the Queen said, "He has, quite simply, been my strength and stay all these years."

But Philip's own strength was failing. An infection in March 2017 caused the prince to need treatment in hospital and, while he had cut back on many public events over the years, he and Elizabeth decided that it was time for him to retire.

At ninety-six years old, and after 65 years of service and 22,219 public engagements Prince Philip announced his retirement in May 2017.

Elizabeth would have to continue her royal duties alone but Philip would still be beside her at home, with time to spend doing things he loved, such as getting into the countryside and spending time with his five (later ten!) great-grandchildren.

A Year Like no Other

When Elizabeth celebrated New Year's Eve at Sandringham in 2019, she could not have known that the following year would be one of the toughest both she and the country had faced since the beginning of her reign.

It hadn't been an easy Christmas. Four days before, Prince Philip was rushed to hospital in a helicopter. Doctors reassured Elizabeth that it was a precaution and that it was to monitor a condition he had had for some time. Elizabeth had not visited Philip in hospital, although she wanted to see him very much. Elizabeth knew the planning and security needed for one of her visits could prevent other patients from seeing their loved ones before Christmas.

Elizabeth was relieved when he was released on Christmas Eve and able to spend the holiday with the family.

Troubling Stories

As the year 2020 began, stories about a new virus named COVID-19 or 'the coronavirus' which had originated in China, dominated the news. The virus was beginning to spread across Europe but in spite of the threat, few feared what was to come.

As well as the virus, another story, closer to home, filled the front pages. The story concerned Elizabeth's grandson, Harry, and his wife Meghan, whom he had married in 2018. On 8 January 2020, Harry and Meghan issued a statement saying that they were stepping away from being senior royals to start a new and independent life with their son Archie in

North America. The news came as a surprise to Elizabeth and was a difficult blow. After negotiating with the couple as to how their new way of living would work with the family, Elizabeth issued a statement.

"HARRY, MEGHAN AND ARCHIE WILL ALWAYS BE MUCH-LOVED MEMBERS OF MY FAMILY ... I WANT TO THANK THEM FOR ALL THEIR DEDICATED WORK ACROSS THIS COUNTRY, THE COMMONWEALTH AND BEYOND."

Queen Elizabeth II, 2020

The COVID-19 Pandemic

But worse was to come. The COVID-19 virus was spreading fast, and soon hospitals were overwhelmed with patients suffering from the disease. By March 2020 it became clear that the government needed to act to stop it. Elizabeth was kept up to date with the government's plan in her regular audiences with Prime Minister Boris Johnson. The government wanted to ask people to stay home. Their plan was to lock the country down to stop those with the virus from infecting other people. This meant there were to be no large gatherings, theatres, gyms and restaurants were shut, people who could work from home were asked to do so and schools were closed to allow children to learn at home. The plan called on everyone to do their bit to help, and that included Elizabeth.

Boris Johnson

Just as she had at the outbreak of war in 1939, Elizabeth sought the safety of Windsor Castle, this time with Philip.

"AS PHILIP AND I ARRIVE AT WINDSOR TODAY, WE KNOW THAT MANY INDIVIDUALS AND FAMILIES ACROSS THE UNITED KINGDOM, AND AROUND THE WORLD, ARE ENTERING A PERIOD OF GREAT CONCERN AND UNCERTAINTY. WE ARE ALL BEING ADVISED TO CHANGE OUR NORMAL ROUTINES AND REGULAR PATTERNS OF LIFE FOR THE GREATER GOOD OF

THE COMMUNITIES WE LIVE
IN AND, IN PARTICULAR,
TO PROTECT THE MOST
VULNERABLE WITHIN THEM.
AT TIMES SUCH AS THESE,
I AM REMINDED THAT OUR
NATION'S HISTORY HAS
BEEN FORGED BY PEOPLE
AND COMMUNITIES COMING
TOGETHER TO WORK AS
ONE, CONCENTRATING OUR
COMBINED EFFORTS WITH A
FOCUS ON THE COMMON GOAL."

Queen Elizabeth II, 2020

As well as offering people reassurance, Elizabeth changed her routine. The palace announced that nearly all of the events Elizabeth and the Royal Family were due to take part in were either cancelled, or would be held virtually, and as the year went on regular annual events, such as The Trooping of the Colour, the State Opening of Parliament and VE Day Celebrations were cancelled too.

Elizabeth received her red boxes as usual and followed developments with interest, but her weekly audiences with the prime minister, which usually took place in person, were held over the telephone.

Elizabeth's family had to change their schedules, and looked to find ways they could help people. Elizabeth's grandson William and his wife Catherine put their support behind Public Health England's Every Mind Matters campaign, to help people manage the effect COVID-19 had on their lives and on their mental health. The Every Mind Matters campaign gave people ways to look after their mental wellbeing and cope with the stress caused by isolation, money problems and worrying about loved ones, and provided support for frontline workers dealing with the long hours and difficult conditions serving in hospitals.

William

Many people hoped that they would be able to return to normal life soon, and that by Christmas they would be able to gather with their families again. But as the year went on it became clear that wouldn't be possible. This meant many people faced spending Christmas alone. Elizabeth used her Christmas message to offer comfort to them.

"OF COURSE, FOR MANY, THIS TIME OF YEAR WILL BE TINGED WITH SADNESS

"- SOME MOURNING THE LOSS OF THOSE DEAR TO THEM AND OTHERS MISSING FRIENDS AND FAMILY MEMBERS DISTANCED FOR SAFETY, WHEN ALL THEY REALLY WANT FOR CHRISTMAS IS A SIMPLE HUG OR A SQUEEZE OF THE HAND ... IF YOU ARE AMONG THEM, YOU ARE NOT ALONE, AND LET ME ASSURE YOU OF MY THOUGHTS AND PRAYERS."

Queen Elizabeth II, 2020

As always, in the time of great crisis Elizabeth did what she could to comfort people and let them know that she was there to support them. Elizabeth knew what it was like to be separated from family and what it was like to lose a loved one. Elizabeth also knew that it wouldn't be long until she lost someone she loved very much indeed.

The End of a Great Team

On 9 April 2021, Elizabeth's husband, Prince Philip, died at Windsor Castle. Prince Philip was ninety-nine years old and palace doctors gave the cause of death as 'old age'. During his lifetime Prince Philip served bravely in the Second World War. He had been the head of hundreds of charities and supported and encouraged thousands of young people to get outdoors and to volunteer in their communities with 'The Duke of Edinburgh International Award Scheme'. But Prince Philip was not loved by everyone. Philip was known to have a quick temper and a sense of humour that caused offence. Many people overlooked these shortcomings because of his service to the country and the way he stood beside Elizabeth and supported her in her duty since she became queen.

Duke of Edinburgh

Before he died, Prince Philip had asked not to have a big funeral, and whatever anyone else or Elizabeth may have had planned, restrictions in place to stop the spread of COVID-19 meant Philip got his wish. Government rules meant that only thirty people were able to attend the service. Elizabeth sat alone at the service, as she said goodbye to her 'strength and stay' in St George's Chapel at Windsor Castle.

Keeping her Promise

On 21 April 2021, just four days after Philip's funeral, Elizabeth saw her ninety-fifth birthday, but unlike other birthdays, Elizabeth spent the day with select family at Windsor Castle. For Elizabeth, it was not a day of celebration, but a time of sadness. People all over the world, sent their best wishes to the Elizabeth and her family.

"WHILE AS A FAMILY WE ARE IN A PERIOD OF GREAT SADNESS, IT HAS BEEN A COMFORT TO US ALL TO SEE AND TO HEAR THE TRIBUTES PAID TO MY HUSBAND, FROM THOSE WITHIN THE UNITED KINGDOM, THE COMMONWEALTH AND AROUND THE WORLD."

Queen Elizabeth II, 2021

Elizabeth may have had to sit alone in the chapel but she was not alone in her life. Not only did she have the support of her family, she had the support of the nation and all the members of the Commonwealth of Nations. After taking two weeks off official duties as a period of mourning, Elizabeth returned to her work, hosting virtual audiences with ambassadors from Latvia and the Ivory Coast. Elizabeth was deeply sad about the loss of her husband, but once again she found the strength to carry on and do what her country needed her to do.

Through triumphs and tragedies, celebrations and scandals Elizabeth kept a promise she had made in a speech over the radio to mark her twenty-first birthday. In this speech, Elizabeth declared that she intended to devote her 'whole life, whether it be long or short' to serving both the United Kingdom and the Commonwealth and she has lived up to that promise ever since.

A LASTING LEGACY

Since Elizabeth was born, the world has changed at a faster pace than ever before. Elizabeth has witnessed world conflicts, political upheaval, natural disasters, and fights for progress. Elizabeth has also witnessed unparalleled technological innovation, from the first television broadcasts to the invention of the internet and the development of the smartphone. Elizabeth's legacy is her ability to adapt to these changes while remaining a symbol of consistency and stability.

As well as adapting to these changes, Elizabeth has embraced many of them in her work, from the early days of television and social media, sending her first Tweet™ in 2014, to her audiences sometimes being conducted via Facetime™ and Skype™.

Developments in travel have allowed Elizabeth to visit more countries than any other monarch.

During her reign Elizabeth has visited more than 120 countries and met with hundreds of foreign leaders including thirteen presidents of the United States. As well as meeting leaders, Elizabeth had met ordinary people too during the walkabouts she pioneered in 1970.

A Leader Among Leaders

Elizabeth's long reign has meant she has seen many other leaders come and go, making her a leader among leaders. During her time as queen, Elizabeth has worked with fourteen British prime ministers, from Sir Winston Churchill when she came to the throne in 1952 to Prime Minister Boris Johnson today. Working with this many prime ministers through the years has meant that Elizabeth has witnessed countless government conflicts and crises and come out the other side.

Prime Minister David Cameron said that during his audiences with the Queen he was very conscious of the fact that he was number twelve and that, "She started with

Winston Churchill and she has heard it all before."

When she came to the throne Elizabeth was head of state in thirty-two countries. Over the years, as more countries gained independence, that number has dropped to fourteen, excluding the United Kingdom. These countries are known as 'realms'. As head of state of these realms, Elizabeth has met and has regular audiences with leaders from all fourteen countries.

COMMONWEALTH REALMS:

Antigua and Barbuda, Australia, the Bahamas, Belize, Canada, Grenada, Jamaica, New Zealand, Papua New Guinea, Saint Kitts and Nevis, Saint Lucia, Saint Vincent and the Grenadines, the Solomon Islands and Tuvalu.

During her reign, Elizabeth has met with fifteen prime ministers of Australia, twelve prime ministers of Canada, nine prime ministers of Jamaica, sixteen prime ministers of New Zealand, eight prime ministers of Papua New Guinea and many more.

Elizabeth is also head of the Commonwealth of Nations, an association of fifty-four member countries, including the United Kingdom and the fourteen realms of which she is head of state. Of the remaining thirty-seven countries, six have kings or queens of their own and thirty-two are republics, which means they have a president. Elizabeth holds a meeting for all of these leaders every two years.

Honouring the Brave

As a constitutional monarch, Elizabeth is not able to make laws or even vote, but Elizabeth is the only person in the United Kingdom who is able to give people honours. Elizabeth awards honours to people who have served the country, either by being exceptionally good at what they do, or for outstanding service to their community. Honours are awarded to people at a ceremony known as an Investiture. Members of the public can nominate people who they believe deserve an award; who receives an award is decided by the Cabinet Office.

The most famous honours Elizabeth can give out are knighthoods, OBEs, CBEs and MBEs. Elizabeth also awards honours for bravery, both inside and outside of military service.

A Medal of Her Own

In 2009, a new military award was created to recognize the families of members of the armed forces who died during an act of terrorism or during military operations. The Elizabeth Cross is a silver cross with the national flowers of England, Scotland, Ireland and Wales engraved on each arm.

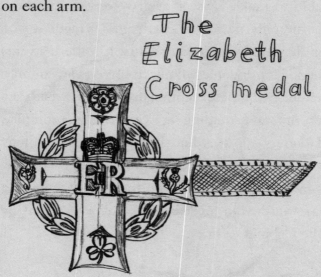

The Elizabeth Cross medal

"THIS SEEMS TO ME A RIGHT AND PROPER WAY OF SHOWING OUR ENDURING DEBT TO THOSE WHO ARE KILLED WHILE ACTIVELY PROTECTING WHAT IS MOST DEAR TO US ALL."

Queen Elizabeth II, 2009

The cross is awarded not just to the families of servicemen and women who have died in recent conflicts, but in conflicts dating back to 1948.

This is the first medal to bear a monarch's name since her father announced the institution of the George Cross in 1940. The George Cross is awarded to recognize exceptional acts of bravery not in the presence of the enemy, such as bomb disposal.

The Victoria Cross is awarded for bravery while in the presence of an enemy, such as on the field of battle.

Style Queen

Since Elizabeth came to the throne in 1952 many fashions have come and gone. In the 1960s many women wore miniskirts; in the 1970s flared trousers, called bell bottoms, were all the rage; in the 1980s torn denim and punk styles were in vogue … but despite all of this Elizabeth's style has changed very little and that is on purpose. For Elizabeth being queen means that she should be a symbol of consistency and tradition.

"AN ABSOLUTE CONSTANT THAT IS VERY REASSURING."

Prime Minister John Major, 2015

Elizabeth and her ladies-in-waiting work with designers on her wardrobe to make sure she looks just right for every occasion.

Although Elizabeth's outfits are very conservative in cut and style, they are often very bright and teamed with a matching hat; this is so Elizabeth can be seen easily among a crowd and in photographs.

Elizabeth is also nearly always seen carrying a handbag. Elizabeth's handbags are very useful. Not only do they finish off her outfit and have room for all her essentials, Elizabeth uses her handbags to send secret messages to her staff. When on official visits, Elizabeth has to talk to lots of people and, like anyone, Elizabeth enjoys talking to some people more than others. To signal to her ladies-in-waiting that she would like to move along or leave a venue, Elizabeth only has to move her bag from one arm to the other or place it on the ground, for her ladies-in-waiting to whisk her away.

Securing the Next in Line

As well serving the United Kingdom and the Commonwealth, Elizabeth's job as queen was to make sure the monarchy continued long after she was gone. Elizabeth has done this by helping to make the institution more up to date and relevant to people today.

One of the ways Elizabeth has done this is by

making herself and her family more accessible. When Elizabeth came to the throne, people rarely saw members of the Royal Family and very few people ever got the chance to speak to them. Elizabeth wanted to show people that she was a real person, so she instigated the 'walkabout', took part in documentaries about her life and allowed her children and grandchildren to do the same. As well as allowing cameras access to her homes, Elizabeth has allowed the general public access. To help raise money to repair and restore the royal houses around the country, Elizabeth has opened the gates for people to visit and even take picnics on her lawns.

A Woman in Charge

Another way Elizabeth has brought the throne into the modern world is by simply being herself. From the beginning of her reign, Elizabeth has been a powerful symbol of women's ability to lead. When pictured among world leaders, Elizabeth stands out, not only because of her jewels or her brightly coloured outfits, but because she is almost always one of very few women among a sea of men.

In 2013, Elizabeth supported a law which affected who could inherit the throne. Before this law, the crown passed down to a monarch's oldest son, even if he had a sister who was older. This meant that if Elizabeth had had a younger brother, he would have been king instead of her. This new law meant the crown would pass to a monarch's oldest child whether they were a boy or a girl.

Paving the Way

Elizabeth saw her role as a mother as one that was very important to her, not only because she loved her children dearly, but also because her children were the future of the monarchy. When Elizabeth's father, King George VI, came to the throne he wanted to make sure his daughter was prepared for the future that lay ahead of her. He hired teachers and allowed her to sit with him when he went through government papers. Elizabeth wanted to make sure her children were ready, too, by allowing them to help her with her work.

Going Platinum

In 2022, Elizabeth plans to mark her Platinum Jubilee celebrating seventy years on the throne. Elizabeth's Platinum Jubilee promises to be a party unlike any the world has ever seen, to recognize the lifetime of service from a queen who has reigned like no other.

Queen Elizabeth II

TIMELINE OF
QUEEN ELIZABETH II'S LIFE

1926 – Elizabeth Alexandra Mary is born on 21 April at 17 Bruton Street, Mayfair, London to the Duke and Duchess of York.

1926 – On 4 May workers across the United Kingdom take part in what becomes known as the General Strike to protest against poor working conditions and low wages.

1930 – Elizabeth's sister, Margaret is born on 21 August at Glamis Castle in Scotland.

1933 – Elizabeth receives her first Corgi.

1936 – Elizabeth's grandfather King George V dies on 20 January. Elizabeth's uncle becomes King Edward VIII.

1936 – On 11 December, King Edward VIII announces that he is abdicating the throne in favour of his brother due to his wish to marry Mrs Wallis Simpson. Elizabeth's father becomes King George VI.

1937 – Elizabeth's father is crowned King George VI on 12 May. Elizabeth is next in line to the throne.

1939 – Elizabeth meets a young sea cadet named Philip at a visit to the Royal Naval College in July.

1939 – Germany invades Poland. British Prime Minister Neville Chamberlain announces Britain is at war on 3 September.

1940 – The Blitz: between September 1940 and May 1941 the German Airforce drop thousands of bombs on towns and cities around the United Kingdom.

1940 – On 13 October, Princess Elizabeth delivers her first speech over the radio to children separated from their families.

1942 – Elizabeth becomes honorary colonel of the Grenadier Guards.

1944 – Elizabeth joins the women's branch of the British Army called Auxiliary Territorial Service (ATS), and trains to become a mechanic.

1945 – Germany surrenders to Allied Forces on 8 May. Victory in Europe is declared.

1945 – Japan surrenders to Allied Forces on 15 August. Victory over Japan is declared.

1947 – Elizabeth and her family set sail on her first trip abroad to South Africa in winter.

1947 – Elizabeth makes a speech over the radio to mark her twenty-first birthday on 21 April.

1947 – Buckingham Palace announces Elizabeth's engagement to Philip on 9 July.

1947 – Elizabeth and Philip marry on 20 November.

1948 – Elizabeth gives birth to Charles Philip Arthur George on 14 November.

1949 – Prince Philip appointed second in command of HMS *Chequers* stationed in Malta. Elizabeth and the family move to Malta.

1950 – Elizabeth gives birth to Anne Elizabeth Alice Louise at Clarence House, London on 15 August.

1951 – Elizabeth rides in the Trooping of the Colour in place of her father in June.

1951 – In October, Elizabeth takes the place of her father on a tour of the USA and Canada due to his ill health.

1952 – On 31 January, Elizabeth sets off on a tour of New Zealand and Australia, in place of her father, stopping first in Kenya.

1952 – King George VI dies at Sandringham House, London on 6 February. Elizabeth becomes Queen Elizabeth II.

1952 – Elizabeth opens Parliament for the first time on 4 November.

1953 – The coronation of Queen Elizabeth II on 2 June.

1953 – Elizabeth sets off on first tour of Australia and New Zealand as queen in November.

1955 – Princess Margaret announces her decision not to marry Group Captain Peter Townsend on 31 October.

1960 – Elizabeth gives birth to Andrew Albert Christian Edward at Buckingham Palace on 19 February.

1964 – Elizabeth gives birth to Edward Antony Richard Louis on 10 March.

1966 – A disaster killing 144 people takes place in Aberfan, Wales on 21 October.

1969 – The documentary *Royal Family* is aired on television on 21 June and is watched by 400 million viewers worldwide.

1969 – Prince Charles is made Prince of Wales at a ceremony called an investiture on 1 July.

1970 – Elizabeth performs her walkabout while on tour in Australia and New Zealand.

1973 – Elizabeth's daughter Princess Anne marries Captain Mark Phillips in November.

1974 – Princess Anne narrowly escapes kidnapping from her Rolls Royce on 20 March on her way to Buckingham Palace.

1976 – Elizabeth becomes the world's first monarch to send an email.

1977 – Elizabeth celebrates her Silver Jubilee marking twenty-five years on the throne.

1977 – Elizabeth becomes a grandmother when her daughter Anne gives birth to a son named Peter on 15 November.

1979 – Lord Louis Mountbatten killed by a Provisional IRA bomb in County Sligo, Ireland on 27 August.

1981 – Elizabeth is shot at during the Trooping of the Colour ceremony on 13 June.

1981 – Prince Charles marries Lady Diana Spencer at St. Paul's Cathedral on 29 July.

1982 – Argentinian forces invade the Falkland Islands on 2 April.

1982 – After fierce fighting, Argentina surrenders on 14 June.

1982 – Diana, Princess of Wales gives birth to William Arthur Philip Louis on 21 June. Prince William becomes second in line to the throne.

1982 – Elizabeth is woken by an intruder in her bedroom on 9 July.

1986 – Elizabeth celebrates her sixtieth birthday on 21 April.

1986 – Prince Andrew marries Sarah Ferguson on 23 July.

1992 – Elizabeth celebrates her Ruby Jubilee marking forty years on the throne.

1992 – The Duke and Duchess of York, Princess Anne and Captain Mark Philips, and Prince Charles and Diana, Princess of Wales all announce their separations.

1992 – Fire breaks out at Windsor Castle on 20 November causing more than thirty-six million pounds worth of damage.

1996 – Prince Charles and Diana, Princess of Wales divorce.

1997 –Diana, Princess of Wales dies in a car accident in Paris on 31 August.

1999 – Elizabeth celebrates the new millennium at the Millennium Dome (now O2 Arena), London.

2002 – Elizabeth celebrates her Golden Jubilee marking fifty years on the throne.

2002 – Princess Margaret dies on 9 February.

2002 – Elizabeth, The Queen Mother, dies on 30 March.

2005 – Prince Charles marries Camilla Parker Bowles at a civil ceremony on 9 April.

2005 – Four terrorists detonate bombs on public transport in London killing fifty-two people and injuring more than 700 on 7 July.

2006 – Elizabeth celebrates her eightieth birthday on 21 April.

2011 – Prince William marries Catherine Middleton at Westminster Abbey on 29 April.

2012 – Elizabeth celebrates her Diamond Jubilee marking sixty years on the throne.

2012 – London hosts the 2012 Olympic Games in July and August.

2013 –Catherine, Duchess of Cambridge gives birth to George Alexander Louis on 22 July. Prince George becomes third in line to the throne, after his father William, Duke of Cambridge and his grandfather, Charles, Prince of Wales.

2014 – Elizabeth sends her first Tweet™ from the @BritishMonarchy account.

2015 – Elizabeth breaks the record for longest reigning monarch held by her great-great-grandmother Queen Victoria.

2016 – Elizabeth hosts a street party outside Buckingham Palace to celebrate her ninetieth birthday.

2017 – Prince Philip announces his retirement in May.

2018 – Prince Harry marries US actress Meghan Markle at St. George's Chapel, Windsor Castle.

2020 – Prince Harry and his wife Meghan announce their decision to step back as senior royals and move to North America on 8 January.

2020 – Prime Minister Boris Johnson asks people in the United Kingdom to stay at home in order to protect the National Health Service (NHS) and save lives during the COVID-19 pandemic on 23 March.

2021 – Prince Philip dies at Windsor Castle aged 99.

2022 – Elizabeth celebrates her Platinum Jubilee marking seventy years on the throne.

ABOUT THE AUTHOR

Sally Morgan was born in Malaysia but grew up in England. She studied Literature and Classics at university. After graduating, she worked as a bookseller and as an editor before becoming a full-time writer. She is the author of many books including *Dream Big* and the *My Best Friend* series. Sally lives in Minneapolis, USA with her husband and two children.

GLOSSARY

Abdication – an act completed by the reigning monarch, where they formally give up their powers as a monarch.

Ally or Allied Powers – countries formally working together. In WWI and WWII the Allied countries fought against the Axis powers.

Ambassador – a government official representing their nation in a foreign country.

Axis – countries allied with Germany during WWII, including Italy and Japan.

Colony – a place under the political control of another country.

Commonwealth – an international association which includes the UK and countries that used to be part of the British Empire. Other countries are also able to join.

Consort – a person who is a romantic partner to the reigning monarch.

Constitutional monarchy – a type of government in which the monarch shares some power with an elected government.

Coronation – the ceremony crowning a monarch.

COVID-19 – a family of viruses that often affects animals, but sometimes move from animals to humans. COVID–19 is a new virus that affects humans.

Election – the formal process by which people vote to choose a person or group of people to an official position in government.

Empire – a group of people or countries ruled over by one person (called the emperor or empress) or government.

Governess – an out-dated term referring to a private tutor.

Government – made up of a group of people that have the authority to rule a country.

Heir – a person that will legally inherit the property or rank of another person on that person's death.

House of commons – a group of officials elected to the British parliament, they are responsible for making laws and checking the work of the government.

House of Lords – the second group of government officials in the UK parliament. They are independent from the House of Commons but they share responsibility for creating laws and overseeing the work of the government.

Law – a system of rules created by a country that its people must live by.

Monarchy – a type of government which recognises a king or queen as head of state, even though they may not hold any political power.

Pandemic – a sudden and widespread outbreak of an infectious disease.

Parliament – the part of government that has the power to make laws, parliament also oversees the work of the government and represent the general public.

Patron – someone who provides support to a person, organization or a cause.

Prime minister – the head of an elected government.

Rations – the fixed amount of a commodity officially allocated to each person during times of shortage, such as wartime.

Realm – an old-fashioned term referring to a kingdom.

Recession – a period during which a country experiences a decline in economic activity.

Regnal name – the name a monarch uses during their reign.

Reign – a period of time when each monarch ruled.

Republic – a nation without a hereditary monarchy. Republics are usually led by an elected ruler.

Revolution – a united uprising intended to forcefully overthrow who ever is in power.

Sovereign – the ruler or head of state of a country.

Treaty – an official agreement between warring nations to bring hostilities to an end.

Tsar – until 1917, this was the title of the male ruler of Russia. A female ruler was known as tsarina.

INDEX

LOOK OUT FOR

KATHERINE JOHNSON

There will always be science, engineering and technology. And there will always, always be mathematics.

NASA Mathematician

STEPHEN HAWKING

Without imperfection neither YOU nor I would EXIST.

Theoretical Physicist

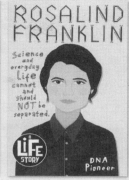

ROSALIND FRANKLIN

Science and everyday life cannot and should NOT be separated.

DNA Pioneer

ALAN TURING

I propose to consider the question. 'Can machines think?'

Computer Scientist

DAVID ATTENBOROUGH

CHERISH the NATURAL WORLD, because you're a PART of it ...AND you DEPEND on it.

Natural Historian

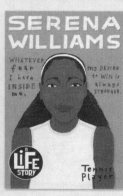

SERENA WILLIAMS

WHATEVER fear I have INSIDE me, my desire to WIN is always stronger.

Tennis Player

KAMALA HARRIS

What I want young women and girls to know is: you are powerful and your voice matters.

Vice President

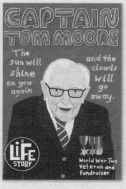

CAPTAIN TOM MOORE

The sun will shine on you again and the clouds will go away.

World War Two Veteran and fundraiser

EMMA RADUCANU

Playing sport, and having to be bold on the court and fearless and fight, it's given me inner strength.

Tennis Superstar